The Usborne Complete Book of

Riding
and
Pony Care

Rosie Dickins and Gill Harvey
Designed by Vicki Groombridge and Ian McNee

Photography by Bob Langrish
Illustrated by Mikki Rain
Consultants: Juliet Mander BHSII and Jane Lake

Managing designer: Mary Cartwright
Managing editors: Philippa Wingate and Felicity Brooks
Cover photo and additional photography by Kit Houghton
Additional illustrations by Thomas Longdill

Additional designs by Cristina Adami
Photographic manipulation by John Russell,
Martin Ford and Mike Olley

CONTENTS

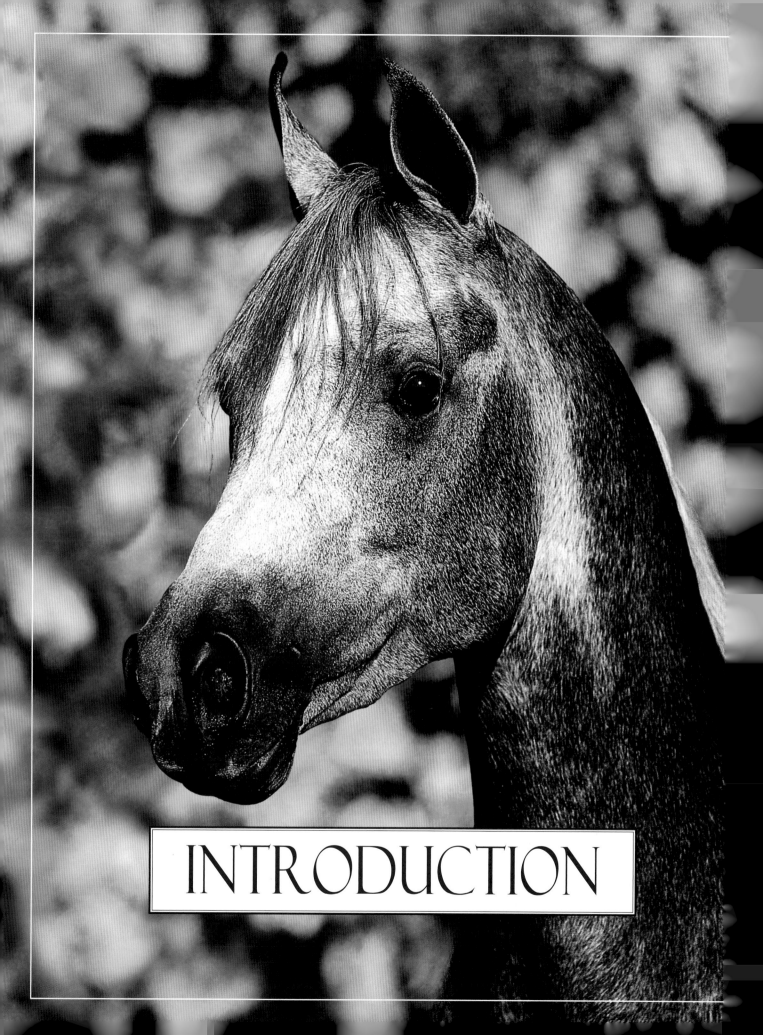

INTRODUCTION

ABOUT HORSES

Horses are complex, sensitive animals, with an amazing ability to build relationships with people. When trained, they willingly allow people to ride them, but they also need a lot of care. This book is an introduction to the world of riding, and to the basics of horse care.

Horse behaviour

Horses are naturally timid. They are always alert to danger, which can make them nervous. Their main defence is speed, so they run away from things that frighten them.

In the wild, horses live in herds. A horse on his own can feel very vulnerable, even if he lives in a field or stable.

A herd has strict rules of behaviour. It has a leader, and a "pecking order" – a system of who obeys who.

As a rider, you take the place of the herd leader, and the horse obeys you instead.

Horse thinking

Horses aren't able to work out what you mean unless you tell them clearly, but they do have an excellent memory. This means that they are very good at following instructions. However, they can learn bad habits as easily as good ones, so it's important to encourage the right behaviour.

A herd of horses sticks together. Horses enjoy each others' company, and hate being separated.

Temperament and personality

All horses and ponies have different personalities. Some are easy-going and relaxed, while others are very nervous.

Horses high in the pecking order may show aggression to other horses. However, it's rare to find a genuinely "bad" horse. Most aggressive behaviour towards people develops because a horse has been treated poorly.

Here, a horse is asserting his position in the pecking order by being aggressive.

How horses use body language

You can tell a lot about a horse's temperament and mood by reading his "body language". This is the way he holds himself and uses different parts of his body. Horses give each other very clear messages this way, and it's quite easy for people to pick up on them, too.

When a horse is feeling angry or very upset, he lays his ears back and swishes his tail. If he is also afraid and tense, he tucks his tail in between his legs, as this horse is doing.

If a horse is excited or very interested in something, he holds his tail high, pricks his ears forward and arches his neck. He may also toss his head around and snort.

A relaxed horse has calm eyes and no tension in his muscles. He may flick his ears around to listen to different noises, and sometimes rests a hind leg by taking the weight off it.

DIFFERENT HORSES

Horses come in lots of shapes and sizes. There are about two hundred different horse breeds, and many more cross-breeds.

Horses and ponies

Horses and ponies belong to the same species, and the word "horse" can be used to mean a pony, too. However, to be called a pony, a horse must be less than 14.2 hands high (14.2hh) at the shoulder; one hand is about 10 cm (4 inches). Horses are taller than 14.2hh and have a different build. Some breeds, such as Arabs, are always called horses, regardless of their size.

Horse and pony breeds

Different breeds of horses vary in size, strength, speed and temperament, as well as looks. Each breed has different traits, making it suitable for particular kinds of work. For example, British pony breeds, such as Welsh Mountain and Shetland ponies, are popular for riding because they are good natured and easy to look after.

The pictures on this page show some of the better-known horse and pony breeds. Falabellas are kept as pets, and Shires are used for farm work or for pulling heavy loads. The other horses shown are mostly used for riding.

Thoroughbreds are very fast and are often used in racing.

Arabs are one of the oldest breeds, and very beautiful.

Quarter horses are the most popular American breed.

Andalucians are an old and famous Spanish breed.

Falabella horses are never more than 76cm (30 inches) high.

Welsh Mountain ponies are a beautiful and popular breed.

Shetland ponies are hardy and strong for their size.

Falabellas are the smallest horses in the world.

Shire horses are among the largest horses and are very strong.

Describing a horse

Horses are generally described by their age and sex. Below the age of one, a horse is called a foal. A one-year-old is known as a yearling. Then, until a horse is four years old, it is called a colt or a filly. A colt is male and a filly is female.

A female horse over four years old is called a mare, and a male is called a stallion. However, some male horses are "gelded", which means their testicles are removed. This makes them easier to handle, but they cannot be used for breeding. These horses are known as geldings.

Markings

An individual horse can be described by the markings on his face and legs. Here are some common markings and what they are called.

Snip *Blaze* *Sock*

Star *Stripe* *Stocking*

Different coats

Horses are often described by the colour of their coats. Here are some common colour names and what they mean.

Grey

White or grey. Lightens with age.

Chestnut
Golden brown coat, mane and tail.

Bay

Brown coat, black mane and tail.

Black
Black coat, mane and tail.

Palomino

Golden coat, white mane and tail.

Skewbald

White, with patches of colour.

Piebald

Irregular black and white patches.

Dun
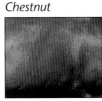
Beige, with a black mane and tail.

Strawberry Roan

Mixture of chestnut and white hairs.

These are Camargue horses which live wild in France.

Young Camargue horses have dark coats, like these two duns and the roan.

As they get older, Camargues become grey, like this mare.

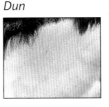

POINTS AND PACES

The term "points" means the names for the different parts of a horse's body. "Paces" are the ways a horse moves. There are four paces – walk, trot, canter and gallop. In Western riding, the trot is called the jog and the canter is called the lope.

The points of a horse

Poll
Neck
Withers
Flank
Forelock
Back
Croup
Hindquarters
Throat
Dock
Muzzle
Windpipe
Shoulder
Tail
Chin groove
Chest
Stifle
2nd thigh
Near fore
Elbow
Off fore
Hock
Off hind
Chestnut
Near hind
Knee
Hoof
Pastern
Heel
Fetlock

Learning the points is useful, as people tend to use them when describing a horse's position or movements. Some of the terms can be confusing, such as "off" and "near". These have nothing to do with the side that is nearest to you. A horse's near side is his left side, and his off side is his right side. When you are sitting on a horse, his left and right are the same as yours. If you are standing facing him, they are the other way round.

How a horse moves at walk

The walk is the slowest pace. It has a four-time beat, which means that you can count "one-two-three-four" as the horse walks. All four strides are the same length, and the horse always has at least one hoof on the ground. He nods his head slightly as he moves.

The sequence of the stride is off hind, off fore, near hind, then near fore.

Moving at trot, or jog

The trot or jog is a rhythmic, swinging pace. It has a two-time beat, so you can count "one-two, one-two" with the horse's stride. He brings one hind leg and the opposite foreleg forward at the same time. There is a moment of suspension before they touch the ground, then he swings the other two legs forward.

At trot, the sequence of the stride is near fore and off hind together, then off fore and near hind together.

Moving at canter, or lope

The canter or lope is a lively, bounding pace. It has a three-time beat, followed by a slight pause or "moment of suspension", when all four legs are in the air.

One foreleg is called the "leading leg". This is the leg which lands on its own and slightly ahead of the others at the end of the sequence.

This horse is leading with his off fore. The sequence is near hind, off hind and near fore together, off fore, then a moment of suspension.

Leading leg

Gallop

Only experienced riders should gallop, as horses easily get out of control at this pace. This book concentrates on the other three paces.

The gallop is a horse's fastest pace. It is similar to canter, but the beat becomes four-time instead of three-time, because the legs which landed together at canter now land separately. The horse lengthens his stride, and there is a longer moment of suspension.

STYLES OF RIDING

There are two main styles of riding: Classical and Western. These styles developed in different parts of the world, so the way in which people ride often depends on the country they live in. However, each style suits some activities better than others.

Classical riding

Classical riding developed in Europe, and it is still the way that most Europeans learn to ride. Originally, horses were trained to be as effective as possible in battle. This led to a style in which the horse could perform precise and difficult movements at his rider's instruction.

To ride in the Classical style, the rider sits upright in the saddle, and uses balance rather than grip to stay secure. The reins are held in both hands, and the rider's feet are supported by stirrups. The length of the stirrups varies – for example, shorter stirrups are used for jumping, to help the rider rise out of the saddle.

Classical riding horses

Many different horses and ponies are used for Classical riding, depending on the activity. For example, Lippizaner horses are used in the most advanced form of riding, called "haute école", and British native ponies are often used for teaching children to ride.

On the left, a Lippizaner from the Spanish Riding School in Vienna performs a move called "levade".

These riders belong to a Pony Club, which encourages correct Classical riding as well as activities for fun.

Western riding

Spanish conquerors introduced riding to America, where it developed into the Western style. As it was important to be able to ride comfortably for many hours, and to round up and rope cattle from the saddle, a relaxed technique developed in which the reins are held in just one hand. The rider sits upright, with long stirrups, so that the legs hardly bend at all. Bridles and saddles also developed differently to suit this way of riding.

The Western style is ideal for activities such as cutting (separating one steer from a herd).

Western horses

This Mustang is a typical Western horse.

Any breed of horse can be ridden Western-style if it has been trained that way. Some breeds of horse, however, such as the Mustang shown above, are more traditionally Western than others. They tend to be small, but very strong, with plenty of stamina. As well as Mustangs, Quarter horses and Appaloosas are typical Western breeds.

How the different styles are used

Many people ride in the Classical style simply for pleasure, but it is also used for many competitive activities such as show jumping, gymkhanas and cross-country riding.

The Western riding style is ideal for long-distance riding and trail riding. It is also the style used in rodeos, American-style mounted games and parades.

As long as it is well supervised, little riding experience is needed for a trail ride like this.

Look round a school or stable before riding there.

WHERE TO RIDE

Once you have decided what kind of riding you want to do, you can think about where you should go to do it. Most people go to a riding school or stable in order to ride.

Riding lessons

Taking lessons at a riding school is a good way to learn to ride or to improve your technique. You will also meet other people who like riding. It's important to pick a good school, so get advice from someone knowledgeable. If you can, find somewhere approved by a horse society (see page 144). Look round a school to see if it is well-run and what the lessons are like.

Riding out

Riding out in the countryside is a fun way to practise your riding, whether you decide to go hacking, trekking or trail riding (see pages 86-93). You can go hacking from a riding school or stables. Treks and trail rides are offered by trekking centres and horse ranches. Again, it's a good idea to find somewhere approved by a horse society or to get a recommendation.

Your own horse

Most riders dream of having a horse of their own, but this is a big commitment. Make sure you know what it involves. Looking after a horse is hard work and costs money, so ask yourself if you can afford it and if you have time for all the chores. If you have not looked after horses before, helping out at the local stables is a good way of finding out what it is like.

A well-managed stable yard

The buildings are maintained in a good condition and the insides of the stables are clean.

The yard is clean and tidy.

The horses look happy and healthy.

CLASSICAL RIDING

WHAT YOU NEED

To learn to ride in the Classical style, your horse needs a suitable saddle and bridle (called tack), which are designed to help you sit correctly. For everyday riding, you can wear casual clothes, but they should meet certain safety requirements.

Headpiece
Browband
Throatlash
Cheekstrap
Cavesson noseband
Loose-ring snaffle bit
Reins

A bridle

A bridle fits over your horse's head and allows you to control and guide him. A well-trained horse or pony should only need a simple bridle, with a snaffle bit and cavesson noseband, like the one shown here.

Different bridles

Bits and nosebands are the parts of a bridle that vary most often. These are different kinds of snaffle bit.

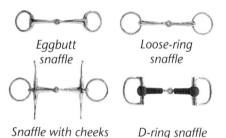

Eggbutt snaffle

Loose-ring snaffle

Snaffle with cheeks

D-ring snaffle

The cavesson is the basic kind of noseband. Two other common kinds are flash and drop nosebands. These stop a horse from opening his mouth and getting out of control.

Drop noseband

Flash noseband

A Classical riding saddle

A saddle fits on a horse's back for you to sit on. There are three main kinds of Classical riding saddle – general purpose, dressage and jumping. For most riders, the general purpose saddle (like the one shown below) is ideal, and helps you sit in the right position. The saddle is often placed over a soft pad called a numnah, which protects the horse's back and soaks up his sweat.

The girth holds the saddle in place so it has to be very strong. It can be made of leather, nylon or nylon string.

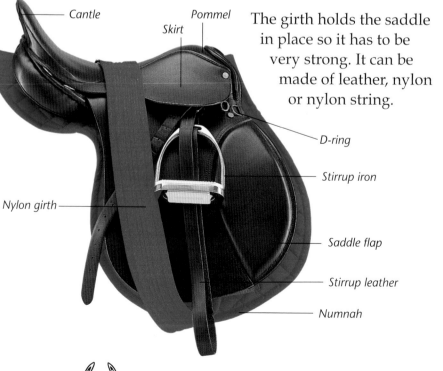

Cantle
Skirt
Pommel
D-ring
Stirrup iron
Nylon girth
Saddle flap
Stirrup leather
Numnah

Martingales and neckstraps

Martingales are items of tack that stop a strong horse from throwing his head up. The two main kinds are standing and running martingales. A neckstrap is a leather strap that is buckled around your horse's neck for you to hold on to. It is particularly useful if you are a beginner, or when you are jumping. A neckstrap forms part of both kinds of martingale.

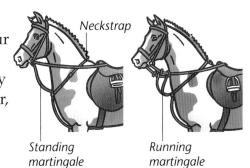

Neckstrap

Standing martingale

Running martingale

What to wear

The most important thing to wear is a properly fitting hat, which meets current safety standards (see page 144). There are two kinds, hard hats and crash helmets. Both must have a chin strap. Crash helmets are the safer kind.

These are some items of correct riding clothing to consider buying.

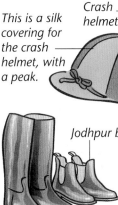

This is a silk covering for the crash helmet, with a peak.

Crash helmet

Jodhpur boots

Riding boots and jodhpur boots are the best kind of footwear.

Riding boots

A body protector is a good safety precaution if you mean to ride fast or start jumping.

Gloves stop the reins from slipping through your fingers.

Wearing casual clothes

For footwear, you need a pair of sturdy shoes with a small heel and a smooth sole. Jodhpur or riding boots are ideal. Trainers or shoes without a heel are not suitable. Wear a comfortable top that isn't too tight.

Jodhpurs or breeches protect your legs from chafing. They are the most comfortable trousers for riding in, but leggings, other stretch trousers or jeans are also fine. Avoid baggy, flapping trousers, or flares.

Formal clothes

Formal clothes – for example, the clothes you might wear in a competition – vary depending on what you are doing. For most activities, you wear jodhpurs or breeches, jodhpur or riding boots, a shirt, a tie and a smart riding jacket.

Half-chaps fit over trousers or jeans. They are inexpensive, and stop a rider's legs from getting chafed.

These boots have a small heel, which help to stop a rider's feet from sliding through the stirrups.

This person is dressed for casual riding.

This rider is correctly dressed for a dressage competition.

TACKING UP

Tacking up means putting on a horse's saddle and bridle. It's important to be able to do this properly, and to be able to take them off again (called untacking).

Carrying tack

While the bridle is still hanging on its hook, undo the throatlash and noseband, then slip the bridle and reins over your shoulder. Lift the saddle and numnah off their rack, resting them securely over one arm.

Hold the saddle firmly, as shown here. If you drop it, you may break the "tree", which is the frame inside it.

How to put a saddle on, or saddle up

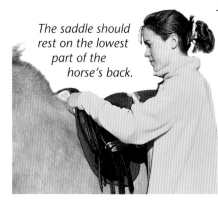

The saddle should rest on the lowest part of the horse's back.

Check the girth all the way around your horse's belly.

1. Tie your horse up first. Then, from the near side, lift the saddle and numnah onto the horse's neck, above his withers. Slide them down onto his back.

2. Tuck the numnah up into the arch that runs along the middle of the saddle. Check that it is resting smoothly under the saddle flaps.

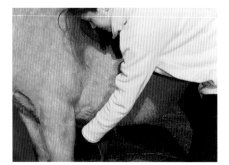

3. From the off side, bring the girth over so that it hangs down. Then, from the near side, reach for it under your horse's belly.

4. Do up the girth buckles, just enough to keep the saddle in place. You don't need to tighten them until you are ready to ride.

5. Finally, run your hand under the girth to check it isn't pinching your horse's skin anywhere. Make sure you do this on both sides.

Putting on a bridle

1. Lift the headpiece and reins up over your horse's face. With your free hand, lift the reins right over his ears and onto his neck.

2. Gently press the bit against his lips. If he doesn't accept it, squeeze the side of his mouth with your thumb. Be careful not to bang his teeth.

3. Lift the headpiece gently up over your horse's ears, and pull his forelock over the browband. Fasten the throatlash and the noseband.

Ready to ride

When you are ready to ride, tighten the girth, one hole at a time. If there are two or three buckles, make sure they are all as tight as each other. Then pull the stirrup irons down the leathers.

Give the girth straps a good tug to make sure they are tight enough.

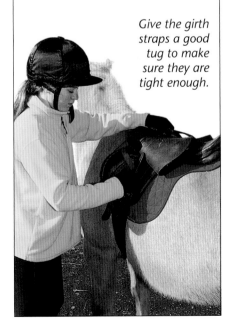

How to untack

1. First run up the stirrup irons. Slide the iron up to the buckle under the skirt, then pull both front and back leathers through the stirrup.

2. Undo the girth. Guide it as it drops so that it doesn't bang the horse's legs. Tuck one arm under the pommel and the other under the cantle.

3. Gently slide the saddle off his back. As it slides towards you, pick up the girth and fold it over the saddle out of the way.

4. To take the bridle off, undo the noseband and throatlash. Bring the reins up to the headpiece, then lift both carefully over his ears.

MOUNTING

In Classical riding, there are several ways to get on your horse, or mount. As well as the basic method shown below, you can have a leg up, or use a mounting block. You should learn the basic method, even if you don't always use it, for when you need to mount without any help.

This rider is guiding her foot into the stirrup iron in order to mount using the basic method.

Basic mounting method

Don't hold the cantle, as this can damage the saddle tree.

Stand on the near side, facing the horse's tail. Hold the reins in your left hand. With your right hand, twist the stirrup towards you clockwise. Put your left foot in the stirrup.

Put your right hand over the centre of the saddle. Hop up and down once or twice, then spring up off your right leg. Swing it carefully over your horse's back.

Try to land in the saddle gently, so that you don't strain your horse's back. Once you are settled, put your right foot in its stirrup and take up the reins with both hands.

Having a leg up

Face the saddle and bend your left knee. Your helper supports your knee and ankle.

As you spring, your helper lifts your leg up to help you into the saddle.

Using a mounting block

Position your horse so he is standing with his shoulder next to the mounting block.

Climb up onto the block and mount, using the basic mounting method.

Re-checking the girth

Once you are mounted, you should check the girth again. Hold the reins in your right hand and move your left leg forward in front of the saddle.

Lift the saddle flap on the near side. Pull the girth straps up towards you and adjust the buckles. If you feel insecure, ask someone to hold your horse while you do so.

Adjusting the stirrups

To check the length of a stirrup, take your foot out of it. If it is the right length, it should reach your ankle when you let your leg dangle.

To adjust a stirrup, keep your foot in it and move your leg back, off the skirt. Pull the top stirrup leather down slightly, then adjust the buckle. Tug the bottom leather down to pull the buckle back into place.

Dismounting

As with mounting, you usually dismount on the near side, though you can dismount on the off side if it's more convenient.

To dismount on the near side, take both feet out of the stirrups. Keep hold of the reins in your left hand to stop your horse moving forward. Lean on the pommel and swing your right leg carefully over your horse's back. Support your weight with your arms briefly, then jump down, landing on both feet.

Be careful not to brush your horse's back as you swing your leg over.

HOW TO SIT

Now that you are in the saddle, you need to learn to sit the right way. Once you are in the correct position, you can let your body relax and follow the horse's movements. Being relaxed makes riding more comfortable for you and for your horse.

Holding the reins

The reins should pass between your little and third fingers, then out between your first fingers and thumbs. Hold them with your thumbs on top and your palms facing each other. Allow the ends of the reins to hang down one side of the horse's neck (usually the near side).

Faulty hand positions

All these positions will make your hands less flexible, and will make it harder for you to control your horse.

Palms up

Hands curled in

Gripping too hard

Hands open

Palms down

Lengthening and shortening the reins

To lengthen the reins, open your fingers slightly and let them slip through.

To shorten them, hold both reins in one hand. Slide the other hand down the rein.

Repeat on the other side, holding both reins in one hand to shorten the other.

When your reins are the same length, hold them in the correct position.

Body and legs

The way you sit in the saddle is called your "seat". Developing a secure seat is one of the most important parts of learning to ride.

Sit in the deepest part of the saddle, with your muscles relaxed, your back straight and your shoulders square.

Rest the balls of your feet in the stirrups, and push your heels down slightly. If you look down you should just be able to see the tips of your toes.

If you could draw an imaginary line from head to toe, it should go from your ear, through your shoulders, down through your hip to your heel.

Arm position

There should be a straight line from the bit, through your wrists and to your elbows. Your elbows should stay close to your sides, but not in a stiff, fixed position. Your arms should be able to swing forward and back (but not outwards) with your horse's movements.

You should be able to "feel" the contact with your horse's mouth through your hands.

Your legs should be in contact with your horse's sides, but not gripping.

Common position faults

This rider is sitting too far back in the saddle, with her legs too far forward. This makes it difficult to balance properly.

Here, the rider's body is tipped too far forward. She is perched on the saddle, instead of sitting deep in it.

This rider is slumped in the saddle. Her feet are pushed too far into the stirrups and her toes are pointing down.

This rider looks stiff and awkward. She is holding her arms much too high, making it difficult for her to sit up straight.

USING THE AIDS

The different methods you use to tell a horse what to do are called the aids. The aids are divided into the "natural aids" – your legs, seat, hands and voice – and the "artificial aids" which are whips and spurs. Learner riders should only need to use the natural aids.

About the natural aids

Using the aids is a rider's way of communicating with a horse. An experienced rider on a well-trained horse can give the aids very lightly, and the horse will understand.

At first, however, you are likely to give aids that are contradictory or unclear, so be patient if a horse doesn't obey immediately. He may not have understood them properly.

This rider is using her hands, seat and legs to direct her horse. She can also use her voice to reinforce these aids.

The rider's hands guide and control the horse.

The rider's legs help to guide the horse. She can also use leg aids to ask him to go faster.

The rider's seat aids emphasize the signals she gives with her legs and hands.

Using your hands

Your hands should feel a constant contact with your horse's mouth. If you increase or decrease this contact, he will think you are telling him to do something different. For this reason, try to keep your hands steady, just flexing gently to and fro with his movement.

Here, the rider's hands are in a good, steady position.

The horse is accepting the contact with his mouth, and is ready to respond to new instructions.

How to use your seat

You may not be aware of it at first, but your position in the saddle makes a big difference to your horse. On the whole, sitting deep in the saddle will slow him down, rising out of it will urge him on. He will also be aware of you sitting slumped to one side, or if you are very tense.

This pony has begun to get out of control, so the rider is sitting deep to try to slow him down.

Here, the rider is in control of the pony's gallop, so she is able to sit quite lightly in the saddle.

Your legs

You can tell your horse different things with your legs, depending on where you squeeze him. The two main positions are called "on the girth" and "behind the girth".

This leg is on the girth. An aid on the girth usually asks the horse for forward movement.

To give an aid on the girth, keep your lower legs in their usual position and squeeze, or nudge gently with your heels.

This leg is behind the girth. An aid behind the girth helps to control the horse's hindquarters.

To give an aid behind the girth, move your lower leg back a few inches to squeeze or nudge.

Your voice

Your voice is useful to back up your other aids, but you shouldn't rely on it too much. High pitched, lively noises make a horse speed up; deeper, slower tones calm him down. Click your tongue to move forward, say "Who-a-a-a," to slow down. Say "No!" firmly to tell him off.

WALK AND HALT

When a horse moves from halt to walk, and back to halt, these changes of pace are called transitions. Horses are trained to recognize a different set of aids for each transition.

Halt to walk

To ask for walk, make sure you are sitting correctly in the saddle. Then, squeeze your horse's sides with both legs on the girth.

As he walks forward, stop squeezing, and relax your hands and elbows so that they "go" with the nodding movement of his head.

Walk to halt

To ask your horse to halt, shorten your reins slightly and sit deeply in the saddle, so that your weight resists the horse's movement instead of going with it.

Increase the pressure on the reins until your horse slows down. Keep your legs close to his sides without actually squeezing. He should stop with his four feet square.

Position at walk

At first, your body may tense up, and you might feel the need to hang on to the reins for balance. Try to get back to the correct, relaxed and upright position you were in when you were standing still.

Listen to the rhythmic "one-two-three-four" of your horse's stride. Let your seat bones relax into the saddle and follow this rhythm.

The rider sits up straight, and lets her lower back rock with the horse's movement.

Keeping him moving

Some horses tend to dawdle if they can get away with it. If this happens, you need to ask your horse to walk with more energy, or impulsion. First, check your reins.

If they are too long you will lack control, so shorten them if necessary. Then nudge firmly on the girth with your legs. As your horse responds, you can stop giving the aids.

This horse is beginning to dawdle. The rider needs to use both hands and legs to make him pay attention.

This horse is responding well to the aids, and walking with plenty of impulsion.

Developing your seat

Once you feel relaxed and secure in the saddle, try crossing your stirrups over your horse's withers. Stretch your legs down and sit up tall. When you put your feet back in the stirrups, you may find that they feel too short. If so, you can lengthen them a hole or two.

Riding without stirrups helps improve a rider's balance.

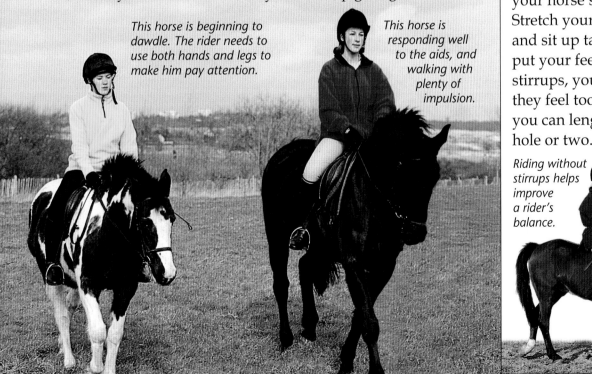

TURNING

For learner riders, the main reason for turning is to change direction. Riders with more experience can also use turning, particularly riding in circles, as a way to improve their riding skills. It also improves a horse's balance and flexibility.

Turning terms

When you turn, it's important to note that your "inside" and "outside" change according to the direction you're taking. Your inside is the side which is on the inside of the curve as you turn, and your outside is on the outside of the curve. When you are turning clockwise, you are riding "on the right rein". When you are turning anti-clockwise, you are riding "on the left rein".

Aids for turning

To turn correctly, as shown here, the rider uses her legs as well as her hands.

Whichever way you are turning, turn your head and shoulders slightly to face the direction you want to go, keeping your back straight.

To turn right, move your outside (left) leg back behind the girth. Keep your inside (right) leg in its usual position. Squeeze gently. With your inside (right) hand, tighten your grip and bend your wrist to increase the contact slightly. Keep a steady contact with your outside (left) hand. To turn left, reverse the aids.

How turning works

When your horse turns correctly, his whole body curves around an imaginary circle. From above, his head and neck do not look any more curved than the rest of his body. If any part of his body juts out from this imaginary circle, it means he is unbalanced.

To achieve a correct turn like this, he needs a lot of help and guidance. This is why you use both hands and legs.

The inside hand, squeezing gently on the rein, points the horse's head and neck in the right direction.

The inside leg on the girth asks the horse to turn, and gives him the energy (impulsion) he needs to keep going.

Contact on the outside rein stop the horse from swinging his head around too far, and gives the rider control.

The outside leg behind the girth steadies and guides the horse's hindquarters.

Common faults

This rider is leaning into the turn. Leaning like this upsets the horse's balance and makes it difficult for the rider to use her outside leg effectively.

This rider's reins are too long, and her inside arm is too far away from her side. As a result, the pony is resisting and refusing to turn correctly.

Riding circles

When you are changing direction, you give the aids, then relax them once your horse has turned. To ride a circle, you need to keep using the aids. Start with big circles at first, as these are easier for you and your horse.

TROTTING

The trot is a bouncy pace, so you will probably find it uncomfortable at first. To get used to it, you have to learn to relax and go with the movement. Learning to do this is one of the best ways of helping you develop your seat.

This rider is riding at a well-balanced sitting trot.

Sitting and rising

There are two ways to ride at the trot. When you sit deep in the saddle and let your body relax into the movement, it is called "sitting trot". Rising up out of the saddle in time to the horse's movement is called "rising trot" (see page 30).

Sitting trot is more difficult to master than rising trot, because you need a very good, steady and relaxed seat to stop you bouncing around. However, whenever you make the transition from walk to trot, you should always sit for the first few strides, so every rider needs to work at sitting trot.

Walk to trot

Before you ask your horse to trot, sit deep in the saddle and shorten your reins slightly. This will give you more control, and also warns him that you are about to ask for trot.

To give the aids for trot, keep both your legs on the girth and squeeze. As he starts to trot, stop squeezing. If he doesn't respond, squeeze again, harder this time, until he starts to trot.

Sitting trot

The basic position at sitting trot is the same as for walk. Relax, sit straight, and keep your legs still. Concentrate on relaxing the muscles in the small of your back, as this will help your body go with the movement better. Your horse's head and neck don't nod up and down at trot, so keep your hands relaxed but steady.

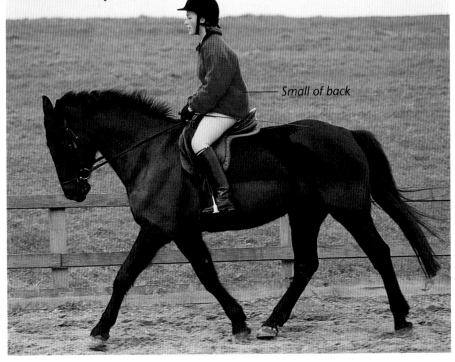

Small of back

Trot to walk

Even if you have been rising to the trot (see the next page), you always return to sitting trot to ask for walk. Sit deep in the saddle. Try to keep your hips still so that they resist the movement of the trot instead of going with it. Place your legs close to your horse's sides. Flex your wrists inwards to increase the contact on the reins. As he slows to a walk, release this pressure and relax.

Position problems

A natural reaction to the bumpy movement of trotting is to tense up. Tension, however, makes your muscles harder and makes you bounce around in the saddle even more.

Bouncing around makes it difficult to balance, so you may tip too far forward or too far back. Other problems are loosening your grip on the reins, or clinging on to them and pulling too hard.

This rider has tensed up. This has upset her balance and made her tip forward, out of the saddle.

To work on these problems, think about relaxing your seat and lower back muscles, and push your heels down.

To help you balance, hold onto the pommel, your horse's mane or a neckstrap with one hand, rather than hanging onto the reins. Keep the reins quite short so that you don't lose control.

RISING TROT

Most of the time, you rise to the trot rather than sit to it. This is because rising puts less strain on your horse's back. Once you have got the hang of it, you will find this more comfortable than the sitting trot, too.

Starting to rise

Once your horse starts to trot, you move into rising trot a few strides later.

To start rising, listen to the regular "one-two, one-two" rhythm of the trot. It can help to say this to yourself before starting to rise. Then, on the first beat, let the natural bounce of the trot push your seat up and slightly forward out of the saddle.

On the second beat, let your seat drop back down into the saddle. Try not to bang down into it – you should only touch the saddle lightly and briefly before rising again.

This rider is rising to the trot as she rides across the school.

This rider is demonstrating a rhythmic rising trot.

To rise correctly, you need to relax and go with the rhythm. Keep your back straight, and your hands steady.

The rising movement should come from your knees. Keep your lower legs still, in their usual position.

The movement up and down is quite gentle. The horse's stride does much of the work of pushing you up as you rise.

Improving your balance

At first, the effort of rising out of the saddle is likely to throw you off balance. This often results in one of the problems shown below. Try holding onto a neckstrap, rather than relying on the reins. You can also try holding the reins in one hand and holding onto the pommel with the other. Be careful not to use your arm as a lever to push yourself out of the saddle.

Here, the rider is pushing herself too far out of the saddle.

This rider's lower legs have slipped back, making her toes point down.

This rider's weight is too far back, making rising difficult.

If lifting yourself out of the saddle seems like very hard work, you are probably rising too high. Try to relax. You don't need to rise very far out of the saddle.

You may tip too far forward as you rise. This makes it difficult to keep your lower legs in the correct position. Try to rise straight, and keep your heels down.

If you keep landing too far back in the saddle, your stirrups may be the wrong length. Check the length of your stirrups, then try to keep your weight forward.

Keeping your horse going

Even the most patient horse may become unbalanced with someone bouncing around on his back. As a result, he may start to resist his rider and his trot may lose its impulsion, or energy. However, trying to give leg aids when you are concentrating on rising up and down can be difficult at first.

The secret to is to use your legs only on the "down" beat. As you get the hang of rising rhythmically, you will find that you can give your horse's sides a quick squeeze each time you sit down in the saddle. This will keep his trot energetic without interrupting your rhythm.

This pony is responding to his rider's aids with a good, energetic trot.

IMPROVING AT TROT

It's good to spend a lot of time working at trot, because it is the best pace to use for developing your balance and seat. Vary your work by using both sitting and rising trot.

This horse and rider are working at a balanced rising trot.

Riding on the correct diagonal

This rider is riding on the left diagonal.

As the near foreleg moves back, she sits.

As the near foreleg moves forward, she rises.

When a horse trots, his legs move forward in diagonal pairs, called diagonals. If you always rise and sit on the same diagonal, your horse will become much stiffer on one side than the other. To check which diagonal you are riding on, place one hand on your horse's shoulder to feel which shoulder moves forward as you rise. If it is the near shoulder, you are on the left diagonal; if it is the off shoulder, you are on the right diagonal. To change diagonal, simply sit to the trot for an extra beat, then rise again.

Circles at trot

Circling at trot is difficult to do well until you are secure in the saddle. This is because you need to give consistent aids for turning (see pages 26-27), with your outside leg behind the girth and your inside leg on the girth, at the same time as staying balanced and in control. You may find it easier to circle in sitting trot, because then you stay in one position.

This rider is rising to the trot on the right rein and riding on the left diagonal.

To circle at rising trot, start by working on large circles, as this is easier. Give the aids for turning with both hands and legs, and try to keep them steady.

It helps your horse to balance if you rise as his outside foreleg moves forward. Ride on the left diagonal if you are on the right rein (going clockwise), and vice versa.

Try to give the leg aids constantly, or at least each time you sit. Either way takes practice, as you need to keep your outside leg in position all the time.

Trotting without stirrups

Practising sitting trot without stirrups is an excellent way to improve your seat. Cross your stirrups over your horse's withers. As you trot, stretch your legs and relax your seat muscles.

Only trot without stirrups for short periods, as it is tiring for both you and your horse.

Keep your horse moving at a lively trot, as this rider is doing. However, try not to let him rush and become unbalanced.

CANTERING

Learning to canter can seem nerve-racking, because you are going faster. In fact, cantering is quite easy to get used to, because its three-time rhythm creates a comfortable rocking movement.

Cantering is an exhilarating pace to ride at.

Trot to canter

In canter, one leg leads the others (see pages 8-9), and you have to give specific aids to tell your horse which leg to lead with. When you are going in a straight line, either leg can lead. When riding in a circle, your horse should lead with his inside foreleg.

The aids

Before you ask for canter, you should be riding at a steady, balanced trot. If you are rising, return to sitting trot.

Put your outside leg behind the girth, your inside leg on the girth, and squeeze with both legs. Your horse should begin cantering on the correct (inside) leg.

The first step in canter is with the outside hind leg, as shown here. This is why the outside leg aid is behind the girth.

Your horse is more likely to strike off on the correct leg if you ask for canter going into a bend. This is because it takes more effort to strike off on the outside leg when he's turning.

More riding terms

When you are going clockwise, you are on the right rein (see page 26), and your horse is leading with his right leg. When you are riding anti-clockwise, you are on the left rein, and leading with the left leg.

Position at canter

Your position at canter should be the same as it is for walk. Sit up straight, with your seat deep in the saddle. Relax your seat muscles and lower back, and let your hips absorb the rocking movement. Your horse's head and neck nod up and down quite a lot at canter, so your elbows must be relaxed and flexible to avoid jerking the reins.

This rider is in a comfortable, balanced and steady position in the saddle.

Common cantering position faults

It is tempting to lean forward, and grip with your knees and thighs. This gives you less control, and may encourage your horse to go faster. Sit up straight, and relax your thigh muscles.

You may get "left behind" the horse's movement, and let your legs slide forward. If so, bring your weight forward, settle into the deepest part of the saddle, and shorten your reins.

Another common problem is letting your lower legs swing back and forwards with your horse's movement. This affects your balance, so concentrate on keeping them still.

Canter to trot

This rider is moving from canter to trot.

The rider braces her seat and increases the contact on the reins.

The horse responds to his rider's aids by slowing to trot.

To slow to a trot, brace your seat muscles against the movement to warn your horse that you want him to slow down. Close your hands on the reins and flex your wrists to increase the contact. If he doesn't respond straight away, relax the aids, then repeat them slightly more firmly. As soon as he slows to trot, relax your seat and hands.

MORE CANTERING

A smooth transition from trot to canter, on the correct leg, can be difficult to achieve at first. However, things will improve as your seat develops. Just spend a few minutes of each ride at canter until you feel balanced and confident.

Transition problems

A horse may sometimes leap into canter rather than changing smoothly from trot. This can be because he's excited, but it also shows that he is unbalanced. Work on establishing a steady trot before you ask for canter.

This pony is rushing his trot rather than starting to canter.

This horse is leaping into canter, instead of moving smoothly out of trot.

If your horse trots faster and faster rather than breaking into canter, you may not have given the aids clearly. Make sure your outside leg is back far enough, and don't give the aids for canter until you are in control and balanced.

How to check which leg is leading

Leaning too far forward to check the lead

At first, you may not be sure which leg is leading. It can be tempting to lean forward over your horse's shoulder to check, but this upsets your balance. Look down at the shoulders without leaning forward instead. The leading shoulder is slightly ahead of the other.

Looking down without affecting the balance

Going too fast

If your horse is cantering too fast, he may be unbalanced or overexcited, which may lead to him getting out of control. You may just want to encourage him to canter at a calmer pace. To slow him down without asking him to trot, sit straight in the saddle and press your weight down. Pull the reins gently, then release them before pulling again. Continue to do this rhythmic "take and give" movement with the reins until his pace has steadied.

This rider is leaning forward, standing in the stirrups, and gripping with her legs. These are all ways of urging your horse on faster. If you want your horse to slow down, sit upright and let your weight sink down into the saddle.

Disunited canter

If your horse is very unbalanced, he may break into a "disunited" canter. This is when the leading foreleg is on the same side as the hind leg that began the sequence, instead of diagonally opposite to it. It is an unnatural pace, and very uncomfortable for you and your horse.

In this disunited canter, the footfall sequence is near hind, off hind and off fore together, then near fore.

If you think that your horse has broken into disunited canter, you need to slow down to trot straight away, then ask him to canter again on the correct leg.

Changing legs at canter

If you have broken into canter on the wrong leg, slow back down to a trot. Wait until you and your horse are balanced, then give the aids for canter again on the other leg. This is also what you do when you want to change direction at canter.

LUNGE LESSONS

In a lunge lesson, your instructor controls the horse, leaving you free to concentrate on your riding. Lunge lessons can help beginners to develop a secure seat, and they can help more experienced riders to iron out any bad habits that may have crept into their riding.

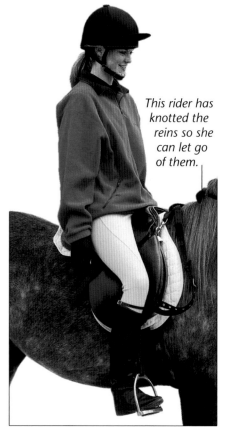

This rider has knotted the reins so she can let go of them.

The rider above has adopted the correct position before starting her lunge lesson.

Equipment

In a lunge lesson, the instructor holds a long rein called a lunge rein, which is attached to kind of noseband on the horse's bridle, called a lunging cavesson. The instructor also holds a long whip, called a lunging whip, which helps to direct and control the horse.

Basic position

The main difference between riding on the lunge and riding with reins is the position of your arms. You can let them hang naturally by your sides, or hold them as if you were holding reins. If you don't feel secure, you can hold onto a neckstrap or the pommel.

The instructor can give detailed advice on a rider's position during a lunge lesson.

Lunge rein

Lunging whip

Lunging cavesson

A lunge lesson

Lunge lessons usually last only 30 minutes, as moving in a circle all the time is hard work for your horse. Start each lesson at walk. This is a good time to do some exercises (see pages 42-43). Then move on to trot. If your horse is supple enough, finish with some work at canter.

Working at walk

When you are working at walk, concentrate on settling your seat into the deepest part of the saddle and relax your lower back. Let your body flex with the movement. None of your muscles should be tense, and you shouldn't be gripping with your knees.

The main part of the lesson: working at trot

Working at trot on the lunge is excellent for your balance. At rising trot, concentrate on keeping your lower legs still as you rise.

At sitting trot, think about relaxing your lower back and seat muscles. Once you can sit without bouncing around too much, take your feet out of the stirrups. Cross the stirrups over your horse's withers to keep them out of the way.

This rider is working at sitting trot. She is still holding the reins, but she could hold onto the pommel.

Working at canter

A horse needs to be very balanced to be lunged at canter.

A horse has to move in quite a small circle on the lunge. To do this at canter, horses need to be very supple, or they lose their balance. Because of this, only work at canter for short periods. Sit upright and let your weight sink down into the saddle.

RIDING IN A SCHOOL

A school is another word for an arena. You often have to share either an indoor or outdoor school with other riders, so it's important to know the rules and terms involved.

Rights of way

A school has two imaginary tracks – one around the edge of the school (the outside track), and another nearer the middle (the inside track). Generally, you should pass other horses left hand to left hand: if you are going clockwise, move into the inside track to pass a horse coming the other way. However, you should let faster horses overtake on the outside, whichever way you are going. So, even if you are riding anti-clockwise, move to the inside to let them pass.

Always move into the inside track to walk or halt.

A school layout

A school is usually rectangular. Many schools are also used as dressage arenas, in which case they measure 20 x 40m. There are markers with letters on around the edge, as shown here. These are placed in the same position in every school.

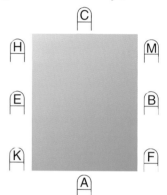

Changing the rein

When you are riding clockwise around a school, you are riding on the right rein; when you are riding anti-clockwise, you are riding on the left rein. Changing direction in a school is called "changing the rein".

To change the rein, you don't just turn around. Instead, you cross the school. There are a number of ways you can do this. You can cross diagonally from one corner to the other (for example, from H to F), or you can ride to the middle of any edge (A, B, C or E), then turn at a right angle and ride across or down the school (from E to B, A to C or the other way around).

This pony and rider are changing the rein by crossing over the middle of the school.

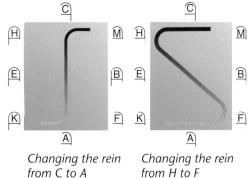

Changing the rein from C to A

Changing the rein from H to F

When you change rein, your inside and outside (see page 26) swap over. At rising trot, sit for an extra beat to change the diagonal (see page 33). For canter, slow to a trot, then ask for canter again with the other leg leading.

Practising different school figures

You can ride different shapes around the school to help improve your balance. These shapes are called "school figures". The usual ones to practise are circles, figures-of-eight and serpentines, shown below. Try them at walk before moving on to trot and canter.

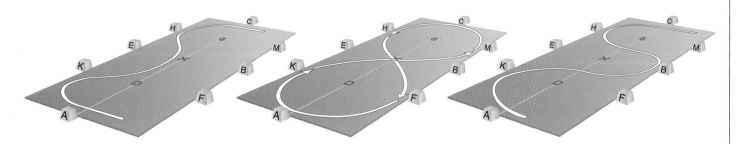

This shape is a shallow loop. When you ride any of these figures, you need to apply the aids consistently to keep the shapes tidy.

When you ride a figure-of-eight, you change the rein in the middle. Ride in a straight line for a few strides to change the diagonal or leading leg.

To ride a serpentine like this, think ahead as you ride and plan which letters to turn at. This will help you to keep your balance and impulsion.

RIDING EXERCISES

Exercises in the saddle are excellent for your suppleness and balance. Do a few at a time, and ask an instructor which are most suitable for you. Always do them in an enclosed space such as a school. If your horse is very quiet, knot the reins and do some at the halt on your own, or ask someone to hold your horse. Otherwise, do some during a lunge lesson.

Touching toes

Lean down and twist your body to touch your left toe with your right hand. Sit up, then touch your right toe with your left hand. You can also do this exercise on the lunge.

Forward and back

Put your hands on your hips, or hold the reins as usual. Keep your legs in position and bend forward from the waist until your chest rests along your horse's neck. Hold this position for a few seconds. Then, slowly sit up again, without moving your legs.

Next, lean right back, until your head rests on your horse's back if possible. Then sit up again slowly, still keeping your legs in their correct position. You need to be very supple to do this. Try this exercise with and without stirrups.

Lean as far forward and as far back as possible.

This rider is managing to keep her legs in the correct position.

Up and over

Be careful not to knock your horse's withers as you swing your leg over.

With someone holding your horse, take your feet out of the stirrups. Swing one leg carefully over your horse's withers, then swing it back. Repeat with the other leg.

On the lunge

The following exercises are all quite easy to do at halt and walk. Once you feel secure, try them at trot, too. Finally, move on to trotting without stirrups. If you feel insecure, don't grip with your knees; go back to working with stirrups until your balance has improved.

Only spend a short time doing each exercise, as lunge work is tiring for both horse and rider.

Body twists like these help to improve your balance.

Hold your hands on your hips and twist your body around to either side from the waist. You can also do this with your arms out wide.

Leg exercises improve your suppleness.

Next, take your feet out of your stirrups. Swing your lower legs forward and back, one moving forward as the other moves back. Then bend one leg and grasp your ankle with your hand for a few seconds. Release it, and repeat with your other leg.

Try holding these arm positions as you ride to help improve your balance and posture in the saddle.

Place your hands on your hips.

Hold your arms out wide.

Stretch up as high as you can with your arms.

Fold your arms behind your back.

DIFFICULT HORSES

Horses and ponies can be very difficult to ride and disobedient at times. Sometimes this is simply because they know they can get away with it; but it can be because they are distressed or in pain. Many problems arise as a result of bad riding.

Napping

Napping is when a horse won't do what his rider wants him to. This may mean refusing to go forwards, refusing to leave other horses, or turning to head for home.

A horse may nap because he's in pain, so he should be checked by a vet. He may also be afraid, confused, or simply playing up. For all these problems, he needs confident riding and possibly some retraining.

Pulling and jogging

Some horses constantly throw their heads around, yanking the reins from their rider's hands. Others pull, and jog on the spot instead of walking calmly. A common cause for pulling and jogging is painful teeth, so they should be checked by an expert.

It's also common for a horse to get wound up if his rider is tense, although some horses just pull when they are excited and want to go faster. If a horse does this all the time, even if he has an experienced rider, he may not be getting enough exercise.

These ponies are overexcited, and are proving difficult to manage.

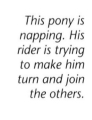

This pony is napping. His rider is trying to make him turn and join the others.

Shying

Shying is when a horse swerves or jumps away from something frightening. It is a natural reaction, so let him investigate and sniff the scary object.

If a horse shies frequently, he should be ridden by a calm, strong rider, who is able to urge him past whatever frightens him. It can also help to ride out with a calmer horse.

When a horse approaches a spooky object, the rider should try to turn his head away from it and ride him forward strongly.

When a horse bolts

Bolting is when a horse runs away with his rider, usually because something has scared him. If he does it often, it may be because he's in pain, so he should be checked over by a vet.

If your horse bolts, the best thing to do is sit still. Avoid doing anything which will scare him more. Screaming or standing in the stirrups will make things worse. If you can, try to turn him in a big circle to slow him down. Give and take with the reins until he calms down.

The rider gives with the reins...

...then pulls, then gives again.

Bucking

Horses sometimes buck out of high spirits, which is nothing to worry about. If a horse bucks often, he may be in pain, so his saddle and back should be checked by an expert.

Horses may learn that bucking is a good way to get rid of their rider. In this case, the rider should sit deep in the saddle and try to keep the horse's head up.

This rider is trying to keep her horse's head up as he bucks.

Rearing

Rearing is a very serious problem that should only be dealt with by an expert. If a horse rears when you are riding him, lean forward to stop him falling over backwards.

Only a very experienced rider should ride a horse that rears like this.

FALLING OFF

Most riders fall off at some point, particularly while they are learning to ride. Here are some tips on how to avoid falling off and how to avoid injuring yourself if you do fall.

Avoiding injury

Any fall carries a risk of injury, but you can reduce the risk by wearing protective clothing. You should always wear a riding helmet and, if you are jumping, wear a body protector as well. Both helmet and protector must conform to current safety standards.

The best way to avoid injuries from falls, though, is to stay in the saddle. Practise without reins or stirrups, to develop a secure seat. Always make sure your horse is listening to your aids and be aware of things that could spook him.

By keeping hold of the reins, this rider will stop the horse running away.

As well as a helmet, this rider is wearing a body protector under her jacket, so her head and back will be protected from this fall.

If you fall off

If you fall, try not to tense up. You are less likely to get hurt if you curl up and roll when you hit the ground. If you can, hold onto the reins so your horse does not disappear into the distance. Let go if he runs off, though, or you could be dragged after him.

What to do

If you or another rider have a fall, the first thing you should do is check for injuries. If a rider has been hurt, send someone to get help. Next, check to see if the horse is all right and whether his tack has been damaged. If he seems nervous, reassure him by talking quietly to him.

Falling off can make you lose confidence about riding, so try to get back on a horse as soon as you can.

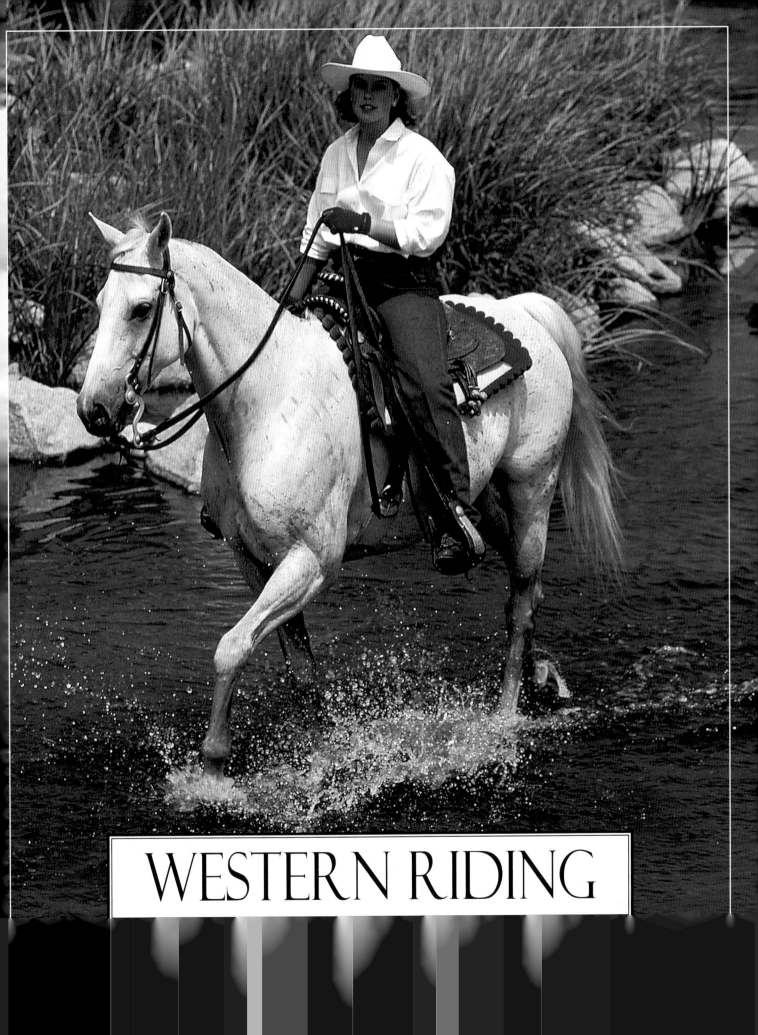

WESTERN RIDING

WHAT YOU NEED

Western riding is a more relaxed style than Classical riding. You ride with long stirrups and usually hold the reins in just one hand. You may find this more comfortable, especially on long rides.

Western clothes

You can dress quite casually for Western riding, but safety is important, so choose well-made, practical clothes. Make sure they are comfortable, too.

Helmets and hats

To protect your head, you must wear a riding helmet that meets current safety standards. Western riders usually wear a broad-brimmed hat to keep off the sun and rain. If you wear one, either make sure it has a built-in helmet or wear a normal helmet underneath it.

Trousers and shoes

Well-fitting, long jeans or trousers stop your legs being rubbed by the saddle. If you plan to ride a lot, you may want to wear "chaps", or leather over-trousers, as well. These give your legs extra warmth and protection.

It's traditional to wear cowboy boots, but you can wear any sturdy shoes or boots with solid heels about an inch high. The heels stop your feet from slipping through the stirrups.

Western tack

There are several kinds of Western saddles and bridles. Different ones are used for different types of riding. As a beginner, you will probably use a general purpose saddle and a bridle with a browband.

The saddle

The Western saddle is shaped to help you sit comfortably in the correct position. The stirrups need to be the right size for you; if they are too small, they could pinch or trap your feet.

The saddle is heavy, but it is comfortable for your horse because it spreads your weight out evenly. However, you should always use a saddle blanket or pad, or both, to protect his back.

High cantle

Horn

Deep seat

Fork

Swell

Skirt

This is a general purpose saddle with a cut-away skirt to make it lighter. Some Western saddles have much bigger skirts.

Side jockey

Rear (flank) cinch

Fenders protect your legs.

This saddle has two cinches, but some Western saddles just use one front cinch.

Some stirrups have tapaderos (covers) to protect your feet and stop them slipping through the stirrups.

Front cinch

Stirrup leather

Stirrup

Crown piece

Browband

Throatlatch

Cheek piece

Reins

Bit

The browband bridle

The most popular Western bridle is the browband bridle. It is often used with a curb bit (see below), but you should use a snaffle bit until you know how to hold the reins.

Curb bit

Snaffle bit

The reins

You can use either split reins or romal reins. Romal reins are usually easier for beginners to handle. They are braided together at the ends, so they won't slip off your horse's neck if you drop them by mistake.

Split reins are not joined together at the ends. This means you may have to dismount to pick them up if you drop them.

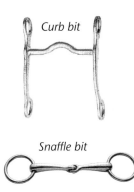

Romal reins

TACKING UP

In Western riding, as in Classical riding, putting on your horse's saddle and bridle is called tacking up. As a beginner, you may not be expected to do this straight away, but it is an important part of learning to ride. Tack must be fitted and adjusted correctly to be comfortable and safe for you and your horse. You should also learn how to take off the saddle and bridle.

Bridling your horse

You should stand on the near side of your horse to bridle him. You need to keep the reins out of the way while you do, so if you have romal reins, pass them over your horse's head. If you have split reins, place them around his neck or hang them over your right shoulder.

Hold the crown piece in your right hand and the bit in your left.

Keep your left hand flat.

Handle his ears very gently.

1. Put your right hand between your horse's ears, so he doesn't raise his head, and lift the bit into his mouth.

2. If he doesn't accept the bit, push your left thumb into the corner of his mouth to make him open it.

3. Next, put the crown piece over his ears. Lift his forelock over the browband and fasten the throatlatch.

4. Once the throatlatch is done up, you should be able to fit four fingers between it and his throat.

Saddling your horse

You should always stand on the near side of your horse when you are saddling him.

Start with the blanket. Place it well forward over your horse's withers and slide it back into position. This makes the hairs lie flat underneath. Put the pad on top, so there is about an inch of blanket in front of it.

The saddle is heavy, so you may need help lifting it.

1. Place the cinches and stirrups over the seat of the saddle and lift it onto the pad.

There should be a gap under the front of the saddle.

2. Push the blanket and pad into the fork of the saddle, so they don't slip or rub.

3. Take the cinches and stirrups down from the saddle and check they are straight.

Always adjust the cinches on the near side.

4. Fasten the front cinch first. Tighten it slowly, being careful not to pinch the horse.

5. The front cinch must be tight, to secure the saddle. The rear cinch should be looser.

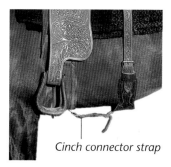

Cinch connector strap

6. Lastly, fasten the cinch connector strap and do up the breast collar, if you use one.

Removing the saddle

Stand on the near side of your horse and undo the breast collar, connector strap and rear cinch. Always undo the front cinch last.

When you have undone them, go round to the off side and put the breast collar, cinches and right stirrup over the seat. Then go back to the near side and lift off the saddle.

When untacking, take off the saddle before the bridle.

Removing the bridle

To take off the bridle, undo the throatlatch. If you have romal reins, hold them in your right hand and bring them over your horse's head. As you do, pick up the crown piece and slip it gently over his ears.

If you have split reins, hold them in your left hand while you remove the bridle.

MOUNTING

As in Classical riding, there is a basic method of mounting which you should learn. It is similar to the Classical method, but easier because your stirrups are longer.

How to mount

It is usual to mount from the near side, but try to practise from the off side, too. Always check the front cinch before mounting. If it isn't tight enough, the saddle could slip.

Make sure your horse is standing quietly before you mount.

From the near side

Stand facing the horse's tail, holding the reins in your left hand. Rest this hand on the horse's neck.

Twist the left stirrup towards you and put your left foot in it. Take hold of the horn or the swell (see page 49) on the far side with your right hand.

Swing yourself up, being careful to clear the cantle, and settle gently into the saddle. Try not to knock your horse as you bring your leg over.

As you mount, you swing round to face the front.

From the off side

This is like mounting from the near side, except you hold the reins in your right hand and use the off-side stirrup.

Facing the front

If you prefer, you can mount facing your horse's head or side. You won't need to twist the stirrup for your foot.

Re-checking the cinch

You should always check the tightness of the front cinch after you have been in the saddle for a few minutes. On a Western saddle, you can't check the cinch when mounted, so you have to dismount first.

How to dismount

It is difficult to dismount safely the Classical way from a Western saddle because the high cantle makes it hard to swing your leg over and jump down. Instead, you should dismount by stepping down. If your horse is too tall for this, you may have to jump down (see page 19), but you should be very careful not to catch your leg on the cantle.

Rest your left hand on the withers.

1. Hold the reins in your left hand and grasp the horn with your right hand. Take your right foot out of the stirrup.

2. Swing your right leg over the saddle and step down. Leave your left foot in the stirrup until you are on the ground.

This is the last stage of dismounting. Notice how the rider is keeping hold of the reins.

HOW TO SIT

Although the Western style of riding is more relaxed than the Classical style, the riding position is similar. In both, your aim is to stay in balance with your horse.

The Western position

You should sit deep in the saddle, resting the balls of your feet in the stirrups. Hold your head up and try to relax.

A good seat is based on balance, so try not to grip the saddle with your legs or rely on the stirrups.

Adjusting the stirrups

To check the length of your stirrups, stand in them. Your seat should be two or three inches above the saddle. If you need to alter a stirrup, dismount and lift up the fender. Undo the buckles on the stirrup leather and refasten it on the new holes.

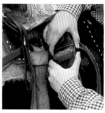

Let your joints stay supple.

Keep your back straight and your shoulders square.

Your elbows should be close to your sides.

Your knees should be slightly bent.

Learning how to hold the reins

In Western riding, you usually hold the reins in one hand. At first, though, you may want to use both hands, Classical-style. This makes it easier to keep your shoulders straight.

Once you are comfortable riding with the reins in both hands, try using just one. There are two ways of doing this. The method you should use depends on the type of reins you have.

Most people hold the reins in their left hand, but you can use whichever hand you find most comfortable.

Keep your rein hand low and your reins even in length.

Romal reins

Romal reins pass up through your hand and out between your thumb and forefinger. Use your little finger to separate them, if you want. Hold the romal against your thigh with your other hand.

Split reins

Split reins go over your forefinger and down through your hand. You can use your forefinger to separate them. The ends of the reins hang loose, and your free hand rests on your thigh.

Adjusting the reins

The reins should be short enough for you to feel the horse's mouth, but not so short that you pull on it. Holding the reins too short can also make you reach forward and spoil your position.

You can lengthen your reins by sliding your fingers back along them.

To shorten them, use your free hand to pull them through your rein hand from behind.

Things to avoid

Allowing your rein hand to move too far forward makes you twist in the saddle, like this rider.

Never cling on to the reins to help you balance – you could hurt your horse's mouth. If you need to, you can hold onto the saddle horn or your horse's mane.

WALK AND HALT

The paces of the horse are much the same in Western and Classical riding, even if they have different names. The basic aids you use to tell your horse what to do are also similar.

Western aids

As in Classical riding, your main aids are your hands, seat and legs (see pages 22-23). You use your hands to guide your horse and your seat to steady him. Your legs mainly create forward movement. You can also use your voice to encourage your horse. If he needs extra encouragement, you can use the ends of your reins as a whip.

Moving from halt to walk

First, make sure you are sitting and holding the reins correctly (see pages 54-55). Then give your horse a squeeze with your legs.

If your horse doesn't start walking straight away, squeeze again more firmly. When he moves off, try to keep your shoulders square.

Sit up straight and keep a light hold on the reins. Let your rein hand move a little with the nodding movement of his head.

As you squeeze, say "Walk on."

Your horse should take even, energetic strides.

If he slows down, give him another squeeze.

Riding position

While your horse is walking, think about your position. You should sit squarely, with your weight evenly spread. Try to relax your body, so you can absorb his movements.

It's easy to spoil your position by leaning forward or twisting towards your rein hand. This will affect your balance and stop you from using the aids correctly. If you find yourself doing this, try to sit up straight. It may help to lengthen your reins, or go back to holding them in both hands for a while.

Problems

To begin with, you may find the fenders on the Western saddle make it difficult to use your legs properly. This gets easier with practice. It helps to sit deep in the saddle and keep your stirrups long. It may help to practise without stirrups, too.

When riding with stirrups, keep them long.

Try riding without stirrups, to stretch your legs down.

Moving from walk to halt

To halt, brace your seat muscles and let your weight sink down into the saddle. Pull gently on the reins, but try not to jerk them.

At the same time, close your legs lightly around the cinch. Don't squeeze, or your horse may think you want him to keep walking.

If he doesn't stop straight away, repeat the aids. If you just pull harder on the reins, he may fight you. As soon as he halts, release the pressure.

When you give the aids to halt, say "Whoa."

As your horse halts, he should bring his hind feet under him.

Halting like this means he's ready to move off again.

NECK REINING

Neck reining is the term used to describe how a rider turns a horse Western-style. It is called neck reining because your reins act on your horse's neck, rather than his mouth. The advantage of this is that you only need to keep one hand on the reins.

This rider is using neck reining to turn left.

The right rein is "pushing" the horse to the left.

The rider is using her legs to help her horse bend.

Reining methods

Neck reining is completely different from Classical reining. Most Western horses are taught to obey both Classical reining and neck reining.

With Classical reining, you ask your horse to turn by pulling on the left or right rein. With neck reining, however, you don't pull on the reins. Instead, you "push" your horse into a turn by laying the opposite rein across his neck.

How to neck rein

To turn left, move your rein hand to the left. Use a light wrist movement and try not to bring your hand up or back towards you. The right rein will touch your horse's neck and push him to the left.

At the same time, put your right leg back but keep your left leg on the cinch. Give your horse a gentle squeeze. Your right leg brings his hindquarters round, so he bends his whole body. The pressure from your left leg maintains impulsion.

Turning right

To turn right, move your rein hand to the right. The left rein touches your horse's neck and pushes him right. Put your left leg back, keep your right leg on the cinch, and squeeze.

Things to avoid

Try not to move your hand too far. If you do, the rein touching your horse's neck will also pull on the bit and turn his head the wrong way.

This rider is turning left, but her rein hand has moved too far.

The right rein is too short and is pulling on the bit.

Pressure on the bit is making the horse look the wrong way.

Practising turns

You can practise your turns by riding in a circle. Exercising like this helps your horse become more supple, too.

Start by riding in a wide circle. Try to keep the curve smooth and even. This will be quite hard at first. As you get better, try making the circle smaller.

You should change your direction from time to time so you practise turning in both directions.

You can also practise turns by riding in a figure of eight or a serpentine, as shown in the diagrams below.

This horse is circling to the right.

There is no pressure on his mouth, so he can look the way he is going.

Turning exercises

Circle

Serpentine

Figure of eight

Try to use all the available space.

This is good practice for changing rein.

Change rein in the middle of the figure.

JOGGING

The jog is like the trot in Classical riding. In both, the horse's legs move in diagonal pairs, giving a two-beat rhythm. However, the jog is a smoother, slower pace, so most people find it more comfortable.

Sitting to the jog

In Western riding, unlike Classical riding, you sit to the jog. This is because sitting to the jog is less tiring than rising when you are covering long distances. However, sitting to the jog takes quite a lot of practice.

Sitting to the jog can seem quite bumpy until you get used to it, but the long stirrups of the Western saddle make it easier. A good horse can help, too. Western horses are bred and trained to have smooth paces.

This rider is keeping a good, relaxed position as she sits to the jog.

Walk to jog

This rider is moving from walk to jog.

The horse raises his head slightly as he starts to jog. The rider's rein hand follows the movement of the horse's head.

The rider has a good, upright position at the jog.

Wait until your horse is walking well (see pages 56-57) before you try asking for the jog. Then squeeze firmly with your legs. Lean forward very slightly as you squeeze.

If your horse does not obey straight away, pause and try again. If you just carry on squeezing, he may learn to ignore you. Stop squeezing as soon as he starts jogging.

Jog to walk

This rider is moving from jog to walk.

Although the horse is slowing down, he should keep up impulsion.

The horse lowers his head slightly, and the rider's rein hand follows.

To bring your horse back to a walk, brace your seat muscles and pull gently on the reins. At the same time, close your legs lightly around the cinch.

If he does not come back to a walk straight away, pause and then repeat the aids more firmly. Release the pressure on the reins as soon as he stops jogging.

At the jog

To sit securely, you need to be in balance with your horse. Sit deep in the saddle and relax your back and seat muscles, so you can follow his movements.

Your horse should keep up a steady pace. If he goes too slowly, give him another squeeze.

If your horse goes too fast, brace your seat muscles and pull gently on the reins to slow him down.

This rider is sitting securely to the jog.

Problems

When you first try jogging, you will probably bounce around a lot. This is uncomfortable and makes it hard not to jerk the reins. To begin with, you may need to hold the horn of the saddle to help you to balance.

Practising the jog without stirrups will improve your balance. Try putting a finger on the front of the saddle. When you have learned to keep your balance, you should be able to hold it steady in one place.

LOPING

The lope is a comfortable pace, so it is good for riding long distances. It has a three-beat rhythm, like the canter in Classical riding, although it is usually slower.

Leading leg

If you watch a horse loping, you will see him stretch one foreleg forward on the third beat. This is called the leading leg.

Moving from jog to lope

You should learn to lope in a school, with both hands on the reins. This gives you more control. Get your horse jogging well and give the aids for the lope as you go around a corner. If you are turning left, ask your horse to lope with a left lead (see below). If you are turning right, you should ask for a right lead.

This rider asked for the lope on the corner, which makes it easier to give the aids.

Asking for a left or right lead

If you are loping in a straight line, it is up to you to choose which foreleg will be the leading leg. It's a good idea to vary the lead you ask for, or your horse may always lead with the same leg.

When riding in a circle, your horse should lead with his inside foreleg. This helps him to balance on the curve.

This horse is loping with a left lead.

This horse is loping with a right lead.

To ask for a left lead, you turn the horse's head slightly to the left. You keep your left leg on the cinch, bring your right leg back, and squeeze.

To ask for a right lead, you turn the horse's head slightly to the right. With your right leg on the cinch, you bring your left leg back and squeeze.

Position and aids at the lope

As soon as your horse begins to lope, relax the leg and rein pressure. Try to sit deep in the saddle and let your hands follow the movement of his head.

Your horse should lope at a steady pace. If he goes too fast, brace your seat muscles and pull gently on the reins. Give him a squeeze with your legs if he is too slow.

If you change direction and need to change the leading leg, first slow to a jog (see below). Then you can give the aids for a lope with the new lead.

This horse is turning right and loping with a right lead.

The rider is sitting well and looking in the direction she is going.

The horse is moving his legs in a three-beat rhythm.

Lope to jog

To bring your horse back to the jog, brace your seat and lower back muscles. Close your legs around the cinch and pull gently on the reins.

Relax your leg and rein pressure as soon as the horse comes back to the jog. If he doesn't slow down, pause and repeat the aids firmly.

Problems

The lope is less bumpy than the jog, but you can still use the saddle horn to steady yourself. Try not to hang onto it, though, or you may find you end up pulling yourself out of the saddle.

At first, it can be tempting to look down to check the lead but, if you can, try to avoid doing this. With practice, you should be able to tell which leg is leading by feel.

BETTER RIDING

Becoming a good rider, like anything else, takes time and practice. Riding around an obstacle course is a good way to improve your riding skills and have fun at the same time.

Obstacle course

Riding around an obstacle course is great for your confidence and your neck-reining technique. You can build your own course as shown below.

First, practise riding around the course at the walk. Try to maintain a light rein contact. Ride over the logs and around the other obstacles. Work out which hand you feel most comfortable holding the reins in and stick to it. When you are comfortable at the walk, try it at the jog and then at the lope.

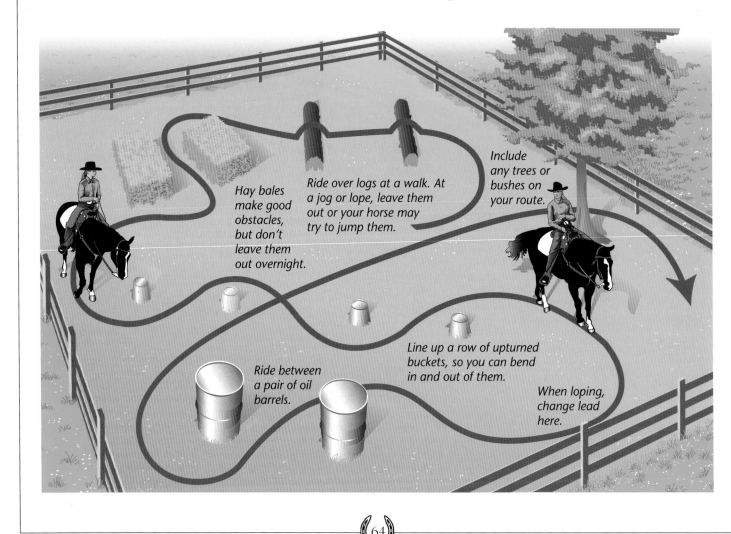

Hay bales make good obstacles, but don't leave them out overnight.

Ride over logs at a walk. At a jog or lope, leave them out or your horse may try to jump them.

Include any trees or bushes on your route.

Ride between a pair of oil barrels.

Line up a row of upturned buckets, so you can bend in and out of them.

When loping, change lead here.

HORSE CARE

GOOD HANDLING

Part of caring for a horse or pony is knowing how to treat him on a day-to-day basis. This is called how you "handle" him. Well-trained horses are usually trusting and willing, and they enjoy being with people. Good handling ensures that they stay that way.

Daily contact

When you approach a horse, he may be startled if he can't see you coming, so never approach him from behind. It's best to approach his shoulder. Put a hand out, palm upwards, so that he can sniff it. Stroke his neck and talk to him in a calm, reassuring voice.

It's important for the horse to see you clearly.

Let him approach you quietly.

When you move around a horse, do so quietly, without any sudden movements. If you need to walk behind him, put a hand on his back so he knows you're there. Never walk close to his back legs, as he may kick.

It's important to show him affection, too. You can do this by talking to him softly and scratching his neck and withers.

Telling him off

When a horse misbehaves, it's important not to let him get away with it, as this can spoil him and make him difficult to ride. You can tell a horse off by scolding him in a firm voice.

If he still misbehaves, smack him on the shoulder or neck. Never smack his head. This can make him nervous of having his head touched by people, called being "head-shy".

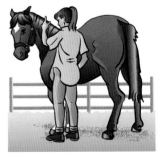

Catching a horse in a field

To catch a horse, you need a headcollar or halter with a lead rope attached to it. A difficult horse to catch can wear a headcollar in the field, to make him easier to grab. It must be leather, so that it will break if it catches on something.

Take a titbit to offer the horse, and approach him quietly, hiding the headcollar behind your back.

As the horse approaches you, or as you get close enough, let him have the titbit. Try not to startle him.

Poll — Headpiece

With one arm under his head, slip on the noseband. Bring the headpiece over his poll. Fasten the buckle.

How to lead a horse correctly

Hold the headcollar rope underneath his chin, leaving about 15cm (6in) free. Click with your tongue and say "Walk on" firmly. Walk alongside him, and make him keep up with you.

If he starts to pull, put your shoulder up against his and pull back to slow him down.

Never walk ahead and try to tug him along, or let him trail behind on a loose rope.

This Shetland pony is being led correctly, with about 15cm (6in) of the lead rope free.

Tying him up

Horses must be able to escape in an emergency, so they should never be tied up directly to a wall or object. Use a little loop of string to tie the rope to, which will break if the horse panics. Tie the lead rope with a quick-release knot, as shown here.

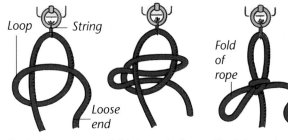

Loop — String

Loose end

Fold of rope

Push the rope through the string. Pass the end around the back of the rope to make a loop.

Fold the end of the rope, then pass this fold behind the rest of the rope and through the loop.

To tighten the knot, pull on the folded part of the rope. To release it quickly, pull on the loose end.

LIVING OUT

Most horses and ponies live out of doors for at least some of the year. It's cheaper than stabling, and more natural. However, horses that live out still need care on a daily basis.

Suitable grazing

Keeping a horse in a field seems simple, but a good field needs regular care to provide enough grass to eat. Each horse or pony needs at least ½ hectare (an acre) to graze, or more if possible. The grass should be healthy, and free of poisonous plants such as ragwort or yew.

A clean water supply is vital, as horses drink about 36 litres (8 gallons) a day. Ideally, there should be a trough which

It's very important that water in the trough is fresh, not cloudy.

refills from the mains water supply automatically. If this isn't possible, fill the trough each day with buckets of clean water. If it becomes cloudy, the trough needs draining and scrubbing out with a clean brush, but no detergent.

These horses have a large field with plenty of grass to graze.

Shelter

Horses need shelter to escape from flies, the sun and bad weather. A high, dense hedge is enough for some ponies, but ideally they should have a three-sided shed. The open side makes it easy for horses to move in and out, and prevents one horse from getting trapped in a corner by the others.

A shed should always have a wide opening.

Dividing the field

If horses live in one field for a long time, the field may become "horse sick". This is when some areas are over-grazed and the grass becomes sparse, but around the horses' droppings it becomes lush and infested with worms. To prevent this, fence the field off into sections and graze one section at a time.

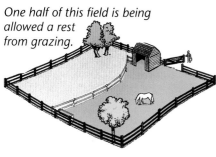

One half of this field is being allowed a rest from grazing.

Feeding

When a horse lives out for most of the year and no one is riding him, he doesn't need any extra food in the summer months and only needs hay in the winter.

If a horse is being ridden regularly, he needs other food, such as horse cubes or nuts, grains or sugar beet, to keep his energy levels up. The amount he needs depends on how big he is, and how much work he is doing.

Chaff is chopped-up hay. It is a good addition to a horse's winter diet.

Pony cubes are an excellent all-round source of energy for a working horse.

Your horse's daily needs

Although a horse will be perfectly happy grazing for most of the day, he still needs checking daily to make sure that all is well. First, check that he is healthy, with no injuries (see page 75).

Make sure that there are no holes or gaps in the field's fencing or hedges. Remove anything sharp which could injure the horse.

Check the field for rubbish. Fill in any holes in the ground, to stop the horse trapping a foot in them.

Take a wheelbarrow and clear up all the horse's droppings. This helps prevent the field from becoming horse sick (see left).

Take the droppings from the field back to a muck-heap.

Preventing loneliness

Being herd animals, horses get very lonely if they are kept in a field on their own. If at all possible, a horse should be kept with at least one other horse for company, but even a different animal such as a sheep is better than nothing.

STABLED HORSES

When a horse is kept in a stable, he needs a lot of care, because he is unable to look after himself as he can do out of doors. He can't graze, roll around or exercise himself, so it's up to his owner to make sure that all these needs are met.

Stabled horses can get bored, so they enjoy being able to look out of their stables and see what is going on around them.

A suitable stable

A stable or loose box should be at least 4 x 4m (12 x 12ft), so that the horse has plenty of room. It needs to be in a solid building, with a good drainage system and a roof that doesn't leak.

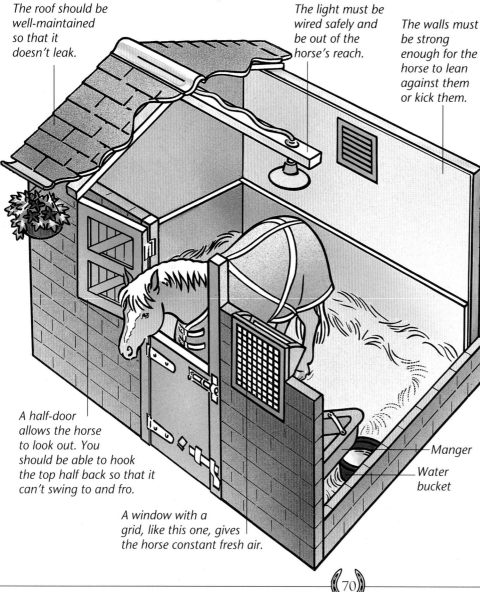

The roof should be well-maintained so that it doesn't leak.

The light must be wired safely and be out of the horse's reach.

The walls must be strong enough for the horse to lean against them or kick them.

A half-door allows the horse to look out. You should be able to hook the top half back so that it can't swing to and fro.

A window with a grid, like this one, gives the horse constant fresh air.

Manger

Water bucket

The floor should be made of something like roughened concrete, which isn't too smooth or slippery. There should be electric lighting so that you can check on the horse when it's dark.

Fresh air is very important. The door should have two halves so that the top half can be left open. The stable should also have windows or ventilation slits that are kept open all the time – you can keep the horse warm with a rug.

The layout of the stable should be simple, with as few fittings as possible. All it needs is a ring in the wall for tying the horse up, a hay rack or another ring in the wall for tying a haynet to, and a manger to hold his other feed.

Food and water

A stabled horse should have a regular supply of hay, so that he can eat when he wants to. If he is working, he should also be fed concentrated food to give him energy. Some of these foods are shown here. Horses need a different amount of concentrated food depending on their size and how much work they are doing.

Apples and carrots are important if the horse isn't eating any fresh grass.

Barley

Sugar beet pulp

Chaff (chopped-up hay)

Cubes

Bran

Maize

Coarse mix

Oats

A constant water supply is very important. An automatic water bowl, which fills up when the horse drinks from it, is best. A bucket is also fine, but it needs refilling several times a day. At night, he should be given two whole buckets of water to drink.

Exercise and grooming

A horse that is stabled all the time needs to be groomed and given exercise, as these are both things that he would do for himself if he was living out. Find out how to give a full groom on pages 82-83.

The right sort of bedding

A horse must have a deep, clean and comfortable bed so that he can lie down without scraping himself on the hard floor. It can be made of straw, wood shavings or shredded newspaper. It's also possible to put special rubber matting on the floor, which means that you need less bedding on top.

STABLE CARE

Basic jobs such as cleaning out a horse's stable and making his bed need doing every day to keep him comfortable. It's important to stick to a routine, so that he knows when to expect your visits.

Equipment

To keep the stable clean, you need a few basic pieces of equipment:

Rubber gloves, so you avoid handling any muck

A wheelbarrow for carrying muck and bedding around

A four-pronged fork for lifting straw bedding

A broom with stiff bristles for sweeping the floor

A shovel for moving large piles of dung

A hose for washing down the yard and stable floor

A shavings fork if the bedding is shavings or newspaper

The horse should be tied up out of the way while you work in the stable.

Keeping the stable clean

A horse produces quite a lot of droppings in a day, so it's important to clean out the stable regularly. When you do this thoroughly, by removing all the dirty bedding and laying down fresh bedding, it is called mucking out (see opposite page). Mucking out needs to be done once a day.

Skepping out means just taking away the droppings. This should be done a couple of times each day.

Skepping out

Skepping out is a very quick job. Either wear rubber gloves and pick up the droppings with your hands, or use a fork. A fork is best if the bedding is straw. Whichever way you use, simply put the droppings in a wheelbarrow or "skep", trying not to pick up too much bedding at the same time.

If you use a fork, shake the fork over the wheelbarrow. The droppings will fall in leaving most of the straw behind.

72

Mucking out

1. To muck out properly, you need a fork, a broom and a wheelbarrow. To keep the horse out of the way, turn him out into his field, or tie him up outside the stable.

2. With the fork, lift all the droppings and dirty bedding into the wheelbarrow. Keep any clean bedding and stack it in one corner of the stable.

3. When all the clean bedding is stacked up, sweep the floor with the broom. Take the muck to a muck heap, leaving any wet patches to dry off.

Bedding down

After mucking out, a horse's bed needs making again. This is called "bedding down". First, collect fresh bedding in the wheelbarrow and position the barrow in the door of the stable while you work.

First spread the left-over clean bedding over the floor with a fork. Then, add the fresh bedding, spreading it out in layers on top. If it is straw, give each armful a good shake to air it before laying it down.

The bedding should be ankle deep and built up around the edges of the stable. This makes it cosy and blocks out any draughts. It also helps to stop the horse from getting "cast", which means getting stuck against the walls when he lies down.

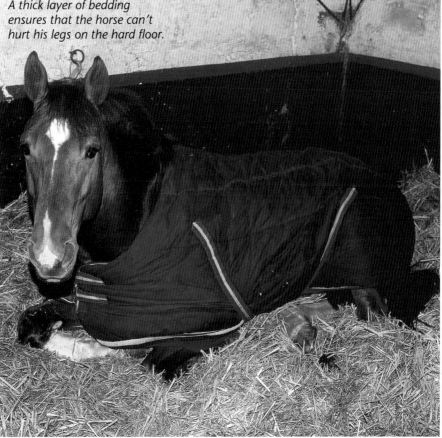

A thick layer of bedding ensures that the horse can't hurt his legs on the hard floor.

Establishing a routine

Horses easily get unsettled and upset if they don't know what to expect during the day. For this reason, it's important to establish a routine. If possible, mucking out, feeding and grooming should all be done at the same times each day. A horse will quickly learn when to expect his visits and will start looking forward to them.

HAPPY AND HEALTHY

Even a well-looked after horse may develop a health problem at some stage. This might be a mental problem, caused by the boredom or frustration of living in a stable, or a physical problem such as having colic or developing laminitis. Fortunately, most health problems can be treated effectively if they're noticed and treated early enough.

Bad manners

Stable life is unnatural for horses, and some find it very frustrating. This can lead to bad-mannered, grumpy behaviour, such as nipping, kicking or barging into people. This needs very firm handling. You should say "No!" and slap the horse on the neck. You should never hit his head, however, as this may frighten him badly and make him nervous of being handled.

You can encourage a horse to develop good manners by spending time with him around the stable.

Other problems

Stress and boredom can cause bad habits known as "vices". Common ones are weaving, when a horse swings his head to and fro, crib-biting, when he constantly nibbles things, and windsucking, when he sucks air into his stomach.

Crib-biting is often a sign of boredom.

How to deal with vices

Vices can be difficult to cure if they are not spotted early, so it's best to work on prevention rather than cure. The best way to do this is to turn a horse out as much as possible, and feed him plenty of hay so that he doesn't have time to get bored and frustrated.

If a horse does begin to develop a vice, you can take practical steps to discourage it. If he starts crib-biting, you can paint his door with nasty-tasting anti-chew fluid.

If he starts weaving, you can fit a weaving grille to his stable door, which makes it difficult for him to swing his head to and fro. There are special collars that fasten around a windsucker's neck, that stop him from swallowing air.

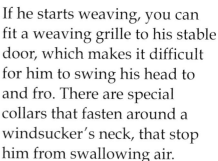

A stable door fitted with a weaving grille.

Carrying out a daily health check

You need to check for signs of injury or ill health every day. Run a hand over his body, particularly down his legs. He will flinch if this hurts. Look for cuts, and feel for heat or swellings. If he's not feeling well, his ears will feel cold, he will hold his tail low and his coat may look rough. If he's in pain, he may be restless, pawing the ground. The whites of his eyes may show, and he may start to sweat.

Check that his eyes are clear, without a runny discharge.

A daily health check doesn't take long, and can help to nip health problems in the bud.

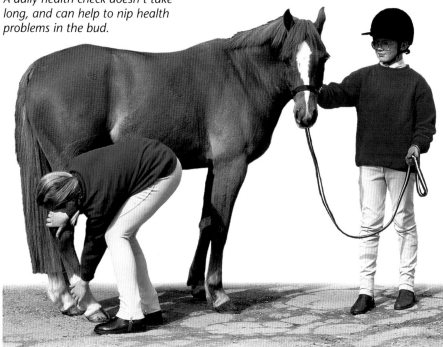

Check that he can eat without any problems and without dribbling.

Check that there are no cuts or swellings on the frogs or soles of his feet.

Common health problems

Colic, laminitis and mud fever are all fairly common problems to watch out for.

• Colic simply means stomach ache. A horse with colic is restless, and may sweat slightly. He may kick at his belly, paw the ground or try to roll.

• Mud fever is when a horse's heels become enflamed and cracked. It is usually caused by standing in wet, muddy ground.

A horse with laminitis

• Laminitis is inflammation of a horse's feet, caused by eating too much rich grass. His feet feel hot, and he tries to lean back on his heels to ease the pain.

The right treatment

Although some problems can be treated quite easily, you should always call a vet if you are unsure about what to do. This is particularly important for laminitis and colic, which need special medication.

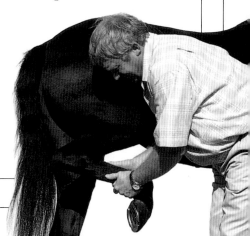

HOOVES AND SHOES

When you ride a horse, his feet have to support your weight as well as his own, so they get a lot of wear and tear. This means it is very important to look after them properly by caring for his hooves and shoes.

You normally hold the hoofpick in the hand furthest away from the horse, but some people find it easier to use their right hand.

Hooves

A horse's hooves grow all the time, like people's fingernails. In the wild, they wear down naturally, but if a horse is ridden regularly, especially on hard ground, they may wear down faster than they can grow back.

Shoes protect a horse's hooves and stop them from being worn down. The hooves still grow, however, so they need to be trimmed instead. Shoeing and trimming are both done by a "farrier".

Parts of the hoof

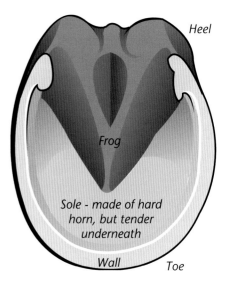

Heel

Frog

Sole - made of hard horn, but tender underneath

Wall   *Toe*

The frog is rubbery and quite sensitive. The wall is made of hard horn, so the horse can't feel anything there.

Picking out a horse's hooves

A horse's hooves pick up muck in the stable, and mud and stones when he is out on a ride or in a field. This means that they need regular cleaning or "picking out" with a hoofpick. Picking out should be done at least once a day, as well as before and after each ride.

1. Stand by the horse's shoulder and run your hand down his leg. Grasp and lift his foot, saying "Up."

2. Scrape out the dirt, keeping the hoofpick pointing away from you. Work from heel to toe, avoiding the frog.

3. Next, check there are no bruises or wounds on the sole of the hoof and that the shoe is not too worn (see right).

4. Lastly, paint the hoof with hoof oil. This helps to keep the hoof healthy and makes it look smart.

The farrier's visit

A horse should be seen by a farrier about once a month. You can help by making sure the horse's legs and feet are clean before the farrier arrives. Have the horse ready in a headcollar so you can hold him while the farrier works.

A farrier adapts a horse's shoes to suit the work he does. For example, riding horses are usually fitted with hunter shoes (see below), and race horses with lightweight shoes. If a horse has a problem with his feet, specially-shaped shoes can help to solve it.

The farrier looks closely at the shape and condition of each foot.

This farrier is rasping the sole of the foot to make it even.

Hunter shoe. The grooves give a good grip on soft ground.

Racing plate. This is very light, to help a horse run faster.

How to tell when a horse needs shoeing

Most horses need shoeing every four to six weeks. You should call the farrier if you notice any of the following:-

• The nails that hold the shoe on are rising up at the ends.

• A shoe is loose – you will hear it clank on the road.

• A shoe has come off.

• The shoes are worn down.

• The hooves have grown too long and need trimming.

Before shoeing. This shoe is old and worn, and needs replacing.

After shoeing. This is a new shoe which has been fitted properly.

It is important that a horse's shoes fit properly, or they could damage his feet. After shoeing, check the following:-

• The shoes should be the right size, and fit snugly.

• The hooves should be neatly trimmed.

• The nail heads should fit tightly.

• The nail tips should be level and evenly spaced.

CLIPPING AND RUGS

In the winter, horses grow thicker coats to keep them warm and dry. Exercise also makes a horse warm, so a working horse's coat should be clipped to stop him getting too hot. When resting, he may need a rug to protect him from the cold.

Clipping

There are several ways a horse can be clipped. Which clip is used depends on how much work he does, and whether he lives in or out. Most clips leave some hair to protect the horse, but show horses (see page 140) may be fully clipped. Western horses are often left unclipped.

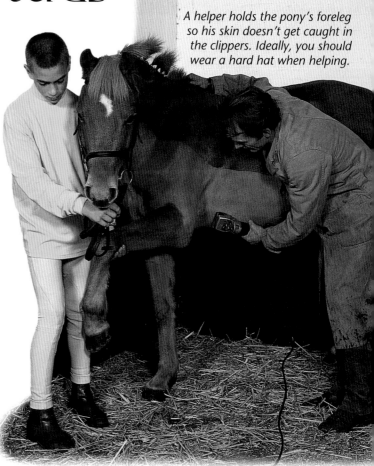

A helper holds the pony's foreleg so his skin doesn't get caught in the clippers. Ideally, you should wear a hard hat when helping.

Bib clip. Only the chest and throat are clipped.

This is the best clip for a horse who only does light work and lives out. He may not even need to wear a rug.

Trace clip. The flanks, belly, chest and throat are clipped.

This is good for a horse who is ridden in competitions but lives out. He should wear a rug when resting.

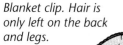

Blanket clip. Hair is only left on the back and legs.

This clip is suitable for a hard-working horse. He should be stabled at night and wear rugs when not working.

Hunter clip. Hair is left on the legs and saddle area.

This clip keeps a horse cool even if working very hard. He should live in and wear a warm rug when resting.

Trimming

Clipping is a skilled job and should only be done by someone experienced, but trimming the hairs around the heels is easier, so you can do it yourself. Make sure the hair is clean and dry. Then use a pair of round-ended scissors to cut it, being very careful not to nick the horse's skin.

Fetlocks. Comb the hair upwards and snip the ends that come through the comb.

Coronets. Trim stray hairs growing over the front of the hooves, to make a neat line.

Rugs

If a horse has been clipped or if he lives out in winter, he may need a rug to keep him warm. When a horse is out in the field, a "New Zealand" rug is ideal. This is a strong, waterproof rug made of canvas or nylon, with a warm lining. It should reach from in front of his withers to behind his tail, and be long enough to cover his sides. It should fit snugly without being tight.

This horse is wearing a New Zealand rug.

Other rugs

There are also several other kinds of rug you may come across. These rugs can be used to keep a horse warm, to help dry him off, or to protect his coat and keep it clean after grooming.

A stable rug is warm and quilted. It can be worn in the stable day and night. It is used on clipped horses.

A summer sheet is a light, thin rug made of cotton or linen. It protects a horse's coat from dust and flies.

A sweat sheet is made of mesh. It lets a hot, sweaty horse cool off without catching a chill.

How to put on a New Zealand rug

1. Fold the rug into quarters. Stand by the horse's near shoulder and place it gently on his back. Unfold it slowly.

2. Check that the rug covers the whole of the horse's back and the middle seam lies straight along the spine.

3. If the rug is too far forward, pull it into place. If it's too far back, lift it so you don't rub the hairs the wrong way.

4. Fasten the straps around his belly. These are called surcingles. Do up the chest straps, but not too tightly.

5. Buckle the leg straps; near side first. Then pass the off side strap through it, so the rug won't slip, and do it up.

6. If he wears the rug all night, check it when settling him. It's best to take it off, shake it out and put it back on again.

CARING FOR TACK

Good tack can be expensive but, if well looked after, it should last for years. It needs to be cleaned regularly, and leather should be polished to keep it in a good condition.

Polishing leather with saddle soap like this keeps it soft and supple.

When to clean tack

You should wipe your tack down after every ride. Use a damp cloth to wipe the leather and rinse the bit in warm water. About once a week, take the saddle and bridle apart and polish them with saddle soap. Check for wear and tear as you clean, especially around the buckles.

What you need to clean tack

Bucket of water

Two sponges, one for washing and one for soaping

Saddle soap for polishing leather

Chamois leather for drying tack

Metal polish and cloth for applying it

Cloth for buffing metal (rubbing it till it shines)

Blunt knife for scraping off dirt

Cleaning a Classical or Western saddle

Remove the girth and stirrup leathers or, on a Western saddle, the cinches. Wipe the saddle with a damp sponge and dry it with a chamois leather. Wet the saddle soap and rub it onto the sponge.

Rub saddle soap into the whole saddle, including the underside. Use circular strokes and resoap the sponge as you go. Then do the stirrup leathers and girth (cinches), if they are made of leather.

Remove and clean the stirrups separately. Lastly, if you use a fabric girth (cinches) and numnah (saddle pad or blanket), clean them. Brush off mud and hairs, and wash them with water and a mild soap.

Cleaning a bridle

To clean a bridle thoroughly, you need to take it apart. Lay out the pieces on a table. Wash the bit in hot water, but don't use soap or you will make it taste nasty. Next, soap a sponge with saddle soap as before, and rub soap into each strap in turn. Then polish the buckles and any metal decorations. When you have cleaned the whole bridle, put it back together as shown below.

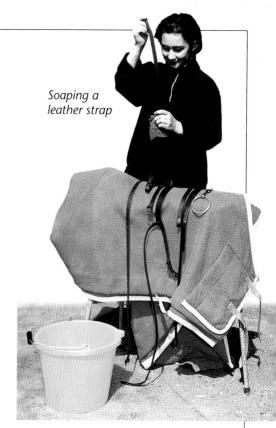

Soaping a leather strap

Taking the bridle apart

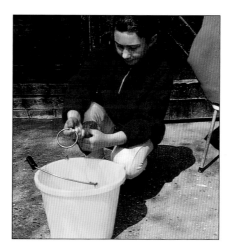

Cleaning the bit

To soap a strap, wrap the soaping sponge round it, grip firmly and pull down with a stroking movement.

Putting a browband bridle back together

While attaching the reins, hang them over your arm like this so they don't get tangled.

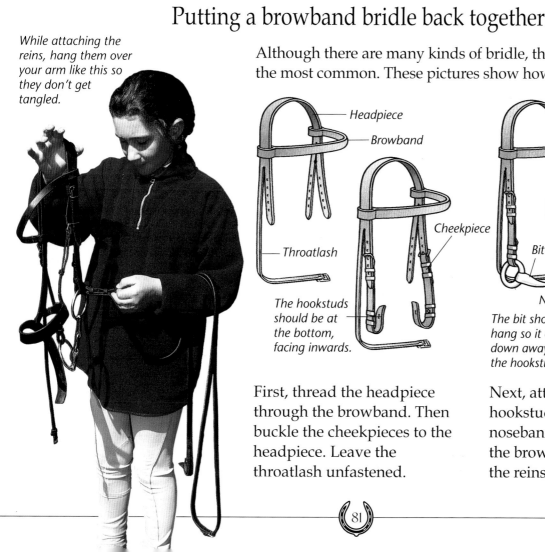

Although there are many kinds of bridle, the browband bridle is the most common. These pictures show how to put one together.

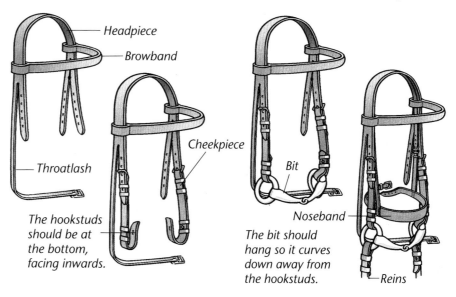

Headpiece

Browband

Throatlash

Cheekpiece

The hookstuds should be at the bottom, facing inwards.

Bit

Noseband

Reins

The bit should hang so it curves down away from the hookstuds.

First, thread the headpiece through the browband. Then buckle the cheekpieces to the headpiece. Leave the throatlash unfastened.

Next, attach the bit to the hookstuds. Then, if you use a noseband, thread it through the browband. Finally, fasten the reins to the bit.

GROOMING

Grooming a horse is a good way to get to know him.

Grooming means caring for a horse's coat. This helps to keep his skin healthy and makes his coat look smooth and glossy. In the wild, horses groom each other, but when you keep a horse, you need to groom him instead.

Grooming kit

To groom a horse, you need the kit shown below. Keep brushes in a waterproof box and clean them every week.

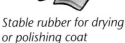
Stiff dandy brush for brushing off mud

Soft body brush to remove grease and dirt

Metal curry comb for cleaning body brush

Hoofpick for cleaning feet (see pages 76-77)

Stable rubber for drying or polishing coat

Rubber curry comb for removing moulting hair

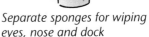
Separate sponges for wiping eyes, nose and dock

Water brush for damping down mane and tail

Horses that live out

A horse that lives out only needs a light groom before riding. A full groom would remove the oils in his coat which protect him from the weather and insects. He may, however, need extra brushing when losing his winter coat.

For a light groom, brush his body and legs gently with a dandy brush, making sure the saddle and girth areas are clean and dry. For his head, mane and tail, just use a soft body brush. Pick out his feet, and sponge his face and dock.

Stabled horses

If a horse lives in, his coat may be dirty from the stable. You can tidy him up quickly before riding out by "quartering" (see opposite page). He also needs a full groom every day, to keep his coat in good condition. It's best to do this after riding. When he is warm from exercise, the pores in his skin are open so the dirt comes off more easily.

A quick groom, or quartering

1. Undo the rug, fold it back and body brush the horse's front. Then fold the rug the other way and brush his hindquarters.

2. Use a damp water brush to get off any stains. Dry the wet patches with a stable rubber. Then body brush his face.

3. Sponge his eyes and nose. Pick any straw out of his mane and tail, and brush them. Wipe the dock and pick out his feet.

Giving a full groom

Only use the dandy brush where the coat is not clipped.

1. First, pick out the horse's feet. If he is muddy, dandy brush his neck, body and legs lightly, following the way the hairs grow in his coat.

2. Next, body brush his neck, body and legs. Use long, firm strokes. Scrape the brush with the curry comb every few strokes, to remove dirt.

3. To do his head, undo the headcollar and, holding his nose, gently body brush his face. Sponge his eyes, nose and lips with warm water.

4. Retie him and push his mane over to one side, so you can body brush under it. Then use a damp water brush to bring it back over in sections.

5. In case he kicks, stand to one side of him to do his tail. Pick out any straw and brush it through in sections. Then wipe the dock.

6. Polish the coat with a damp stable rubber. If he wears a rug, put it on (see page 79) and, lastly, paint his hooves with hoof oil.

AFTER RIDING

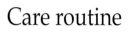

It is important to care for a horse properly after riding, especially if he has been working hard. Following the care routine described below will help him recover from the ride. A regular routine also helps him settle down.

Back at the yard

When you get back from a ride, if it is warm, tie up your horse in the yard. If it is cold, shut him in his box. Then check him over for any cuts or scratches.

Untack (see page 17 or 51), put on a headcollar, and give his back a quick rub. If he is in his box, leave him loose while you put the tack away, so he can roll if he wants to.

If the horse is hot, loosen the girth but leave the saddle on for a few minutes, so his back doesn't feel cold suddenly.

Care routine

First, if your horse is sweaty, dry him off with a stable rubber. If he is sweating a lot, sponge him down with lukewarm water and use a sweat scraper to dry him. Then let him have a small drink and give him some hay to eat while you groom him (see pages 82-83).

As you clean his legs, run your hands over them to check for injuries. Ask for help if they seem hot or swollen. Check his body temperature by feeling his ears. If they are cold, he may need an extra rug. Stroke them gently to warm them.

Next, put on a sweat sheet and rug (see page 79), if he wears them. You can now turn him out or shut him in his box. Lastly, give him water and a small feed, and make sure he is comfortable before you leave. Check his rugs and see that he has enough water and hay.

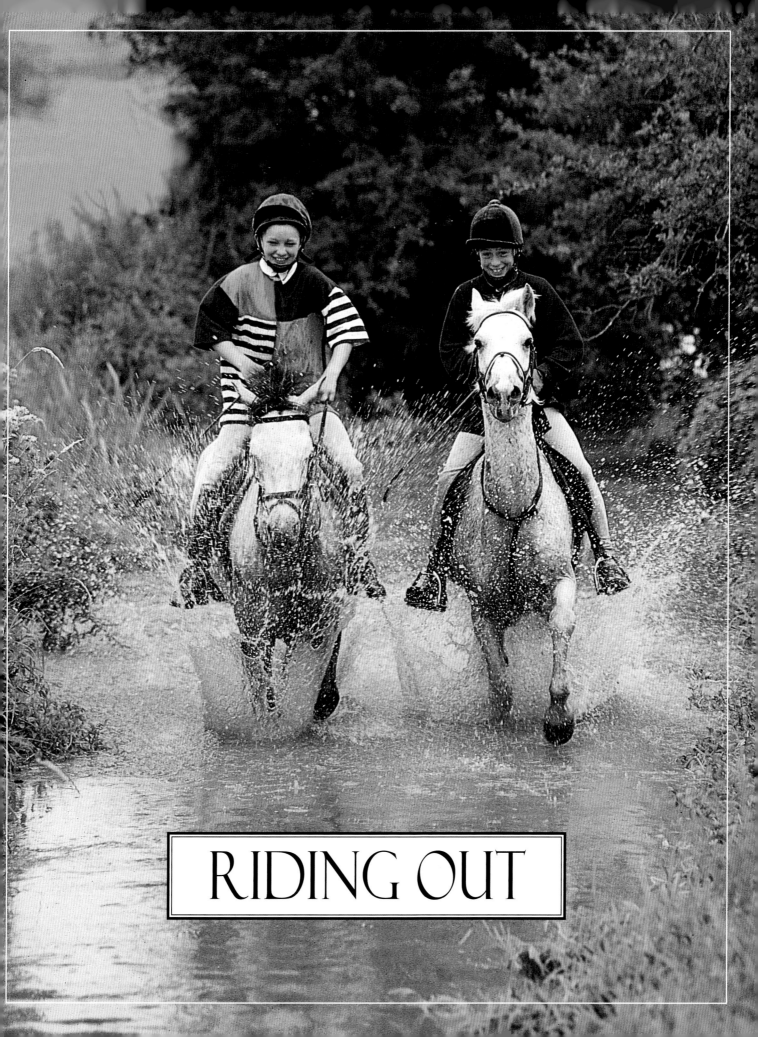

RIDING OUT

HACKING

Hacking means riding out in the open, either along roads and tracks or across the countryside. It is a good way to practise your riding skills and you may well find that being outside the school helps you relax, so your balance and position improve.

Planning

Whenever you go for a hack, plan your route first and tell someone where you are going. Most local maps show bridleways, which are tracks and paths where you are allowed to ride. If you want to ride over farmland or private property, ask permission. If you are riding out for the first time, its best to go with someone more experienced, who knows the area and who can show you where to go.

Riding in a group

If you are riding in a group, try to keep a sensible distance from the other horses. When riding single file, there should be at least one horse's length between you and the horse in front.

Warn other riders if you are going to change pace. If you want to canter, it is better to break up and go in ones and twos, or the horses may get excited and try to race.

Outside the school

An unfamiliar sight or sound can spook a horse.

Most people learn to ride in a school. In the open, it can be harder to control your horse. If he spooks or plays up, be firm and stay calm. He will sense it if you are nervous.

Riding in a group like this is more fun and safer than riding by yourself.

Different ground conditions

Hacking involves riding over different sorts of ground, so you need to adjust your pace to suit the conditions.

If the ground is rough or uneven, let your horse walk slowly so he can pick his way across it. On hard, dry ground, you can walk or trot, but never canter or jump.

Only canter on firm, level ground without holes or sharp stones. Don't canter every time you come to a stretch of grass, or your horse may make a habit of it.

A grassy field like this is a good place for a canter.

Weather

Try to be aware of how the weather affects the ground. In hot weather, it will be dry and hard. Rain or frost make it more slippery. Try to avoid riding through mud. It can cause a horse to strain his legs.

The weather can affect your horse's mood, too. If it is hot, he may be sleepy or lazy. If it is windy, he may find more things than usual to spook at.

Wet roads like this can be slippery, so stay alert and ride slowly. If possible, horses should wear boots to protect their legs and knees in case they slip.

Riding on hills

Going up and down hills is hard work for your horse, but you can help him by changing your position slightly. This makes it easier for him to balance on the slope.

Going uphill

Going downhill

To go uphill, bend forward from your hips to keep your weight off your horse's hindquarters. Allow him plenty of rein, so he can use his head and neck to balance, but don't lose contact with his mouth.

When going downhill, sit vertically and push your heels down to stop your feet slipping through the stirrups. Maintain rein contact with your horse's mouth, but let him stretch his neck out so he can balance.

HACKING SKILLS

Hacking across farmland is exciting, but make sure you ask permission and obey the country code.

Riding out in the open involves different skills from riding in an enclosed school. It is important to know what to do when riding through farmland or in the countryside, and how to ride safely on the road.

The country code

The country code is a set of rules which you should follow when you are riding out in the countryside:

• Always keep to a track or bridleway where there is one, and ask for permission before riding over private land.

• Avoid riding across fields that have been ploughed or planted with crops. If there is no track, keep to the edge of a field.

• Be considerate. If you meet other people or horses, pass them at a walk.

• If you come across animals in a field, go around them slowly, so you don't disturb them.

• Shut any gates you open.

Opening and shutting gates

If you need to go through a gate, you can get off and lead your horse through on foot. With practice, however, you can learn to open and shut a gate without dismounting.

Walk up to the gate, stopping with your horse's shoulder near the latch.

Reach down and open the gate. Be careful it doesn't knock your horse.

Ride through slowly, keeping one hand on the gate to stop it from swinging.

Turn and bring your horse back alongside the gate so that you can close it.

Riding on the road

It is best to avoid riding on the road, especially in traffic, but this may not always be possible. If you do need to ride on the road, make sure that your horse is familiar with traffic and that you know the highway code. It's a good idea to buy insurance against injury and, if possible, take the Pony Club riding and road safety exam.

Until you are used to roads, ride with an experienced person.

Always ride on the inside, leaving cars room to pass, unless you are overtaking.

Road safety

• Stay alert and make sure your horse is listening to your aids.

• Keep to the inside and, if possible, ride on the verge. Walk or trot, but don't canter, even on the verge.

• Thank drivers who slow down. Raise one hand or nod and smile.

• If you want to change direction, warn drivers by signalling. If you are turning left, hold out your left arm. For a right turn, use your right arm.

• If you see something that might spook your horse, wait until the road is clear before you try to pass it.

• If you are leading a horse on the road, keep him on the inside, away from the traffic.

• Wear reflective clothing so that drivers can see you, especially if it is raining or getting dark.

Reflective clothing shows up clearly, even in poor light.

TREKKING

Trekking is something everybody can enjoy, even complete beginners. Most treks are organized on moorland and downland, in parks and through forests, so they are an opportunity to see the countryside at its best.

Choosing a trek

A trek can last anything from an hour to a few days. Some stables offer trekking holidays. Riding schools and Pony Clubs may also run treks. As a beginner, it's best to join a guided trek run by a good stable – try to find one approved by a horse society. If you are used to riding out, you could organize your own trek, but plan your route carefully.

Preparing for a trek

Trekking usually means spending a long time in the saddle, riding off the beaten track. This can be very tiring, so it is important to wear comfortable clothes (see page 15). You should make sure your tack is comfortable, too, and in good condition.

Your saddle is more likely to slip on hilly ground, so do the girth up tightly. On a long trek, it's a good idea for your

Put the head-collar over the bridle or, if you are going on a long trek, under it.

horse to wear a headcollar with his bridle, so you can tie him up when you stop to rest. Leave the lead rope attached and knot it loosely round your horse's neck to keep it out of the way while you ride.

A beach provides a good, soft surface for riding in all weathers.

On a trek

Be considerate when you are riding in a group, especially if you are with less experienced riders. Keep a sensible distance from the horse in front and, if you need to stop, move aside to let others pass. Tell other riders before you change pace, as their horses may try to follow.

Stay alert. If one horse shies, others might copy. If you see anything dangerous, like rabbit holes or barbed wire, warn other riders. Remember the country code.

You may find yourself on narrow paths where you have to ride in single file. If so, the fastest horses should go at the front. Any horses that kick should stay at the back, out of the way of the others.

Taking a break

Having a rest is important on a long trek.

If you are trekking for more than a few hours, you will need to take a break so that you and your horse can rest. Try to stop somewhere where there is water for your horse to drink. If it is hot and sunny, try to find some shade.

Run up the stirrups and tie up your horse, tucking the reins under one of the stirrups to keep them out of the way. Loosen the girth to make him comfortable while you rest, but don't forget to tighten it before you set off again.

You should wear shoes with heels, and a hat that conforms to current safety standards (see page 15). These riders are not ideally dressed.

TRAIL RIDING

By trail riding, most people mean going on pleasure trail rides, although competitive trail rides exist as well. A pleasure trail ride is really a Western-style trek and, like a trek, you don't have to have ridden before to enjoy one.

Pleasure rides

Pleasure trail rides are organized to give riders a good day out in the countryside. A pleasure ride is a great way to improve your fitness and explore your surroundings. Unless you have enough experience to plan your own ride, you should join an accompanied trail ride.

Where to go

There are many places offering pleasure trail rides, so you have quite a wide choice of who to ride with and where to go. Try to find a stable or ranch that has been recommended or endorsed by a horse society, and that offers rides through interesting countryside.

Trail horses like these should be calm and obedient. They have to cope with rough ground and many different obstacles on a trail.

What to wear

You can wear normal riding clothes (see page 48), but be prepared for different kinds of weather.

In cold or wet weather, you may need an extra sweater or a waterproof jacket. If you don't want to wear it straight away, you can roll it up and tie it to your saddle with the saddle strings. Gloves will keep your hands warm. They also make it easier to hold wet reins, which can be slippery.

If it is going to be very hot, you may want to ride in the early morning or in the evening, when it is cooler. In very sunny weather, you should wear sun cream. A Western-style hat will protect your head from the sun, but make sure it will also protect your head if you fall (see page 48).

Competitive rides

Competitive or endurance rides have longer routes than pleasure rides. The aim of the ride is to get home within a set time and with your horse still in a good condition.

The horses need to be very fit, which requires special training or "conditioning".

Riders in the Tevis Cup in the United States cover 100 miles (160 km) in one day.

LONGER RIDES

Most hacks and treks only last a few hours, but a longer ride can provide a great day out, as well as developing your stamina and fitness. A long ride is tiring, but it's easier if you plan it well beforehand.

Beforehand

Make sure you know your route and, if you are riding by yourself, let someone know where you are going and when you expect to be back. Don't plan to go too far at first, but build up the length of your rides slowly.

Check you have everything you need. A map and a hoofpick (see page 76) are essential, and it's a good idea to take coins for a payphone or a mobile phone. You may want a waterproof or extra sweater and some snacks, too.

On a ride

It is important to set the right pace. Changing pace to suit the ground will tire your horse less and keep him alert.

If you do a lot of rising trot, change diagonals from time to time. On good, level ground, a relaxed canter is easiest for your horse. Walk over rough or hilly ground.

You should take a rest from time to time, but don't stop for too long. Make sure you move on before you or your horse start to get stiff or cold.

Going home

Try to finish your ride at a walk, to let your horse cool off. For the last half mile, dismount and run up your stirrups. Slacken the girth, to allow the circulation to return to your horse's back, and lead him the rest of the way.

When you get back, you need to groom and care for your horse carefully (see page 84) to help him recover.

The riders below are taking a short rest to let their horses drink. The horses should not be allowed to eat, though, as they won't have time to digest.

JUMPING

PREPARING TO JUMP

Jumping is exciting, but it can be dangerous, so it is important to be well prepared. Before you can learn to jump, you must have a secure seat and good control of your horse. You must also be sure to have the right clothes and equipment.

Jumping saddle

This saddle is shaped with a "forward cut" which helps you keep the forward position.

General purpose saddle

This saddle is less forward cut, but it is fine for small jumps, riding school and Pony Club work.

Clothes and tack

Jumping often means riding fast, so if you fall, you are likely to fall hard. This means you should wear a body protector as well as your riding helmet.

When you jump, you sit in the forward position (see pages 98-99). Jumping saddles are specially cut and shaped to help you do this.

You may need a jumping saddle if you plan to jump a lot, but a general purpose saddle is fine to begin with.

When you start jumping, you may want to use a neckstrap (see page 15) to help you balance. Holding the neckstrap will also make it easier to keep your hands steady, so you don't pull on the reins.

These riders are correctly dressed for jumping, with body protectors and helmets.

Body protector

This rider is using a jumping saddle rather than a general purpose saddle.

Body protectors and helmets must meet current safety standards.

Developing your riding skills

To prepare for jumping, work on developing your balance, rhythm and impulsion as explained below. Only try jumping when you feel ready. If you lack confidence, your horse will sense it and be nervous.

Balance, rhythm and impulsion

When jumping, you need to stay in balance with your horse. His weight shifts forward when he jumps and, to stay in balance with him, you must move forward too. You can improve your sense of balance by working without stirrups. Practising turns and circles also helps.

This horse is moving with good impulsion.

This rider is encouraging a steady rhythm.

A good rhythm helps you control the approach to a jump. You should work on maintaining a steady pace with a regular rhythm.

Impulsion is also important for jumping. Your horse should move energetically, but must be under control. You can work on impulsion by practising transitions of pace.

Warming up before jumping

Jumping can be hard work, so it is important that both you and your horse warm up properly, as described below, before you start.

Warming up prevents you and your horse from straining any muscles when jumping. A warm up should take about 20 minutes.

Start by walking, keeping your reins long to let your horse stretch. Then shorten your reins and work on the transition from walk to trot.

Then settle your horse into a steady trot. When you are trotting with rhythm, balance and impulsion, try riding some turns and circles.

Next, canter on each rein, making sure your horse leads with the correct leg. Finish with a relaxed walk. You should now be ready to jump.

JUMPING POSITION

When jumping, you need to help your horse by staying in balance with him and taking your weight off his back. You do this by changing your position as he jumps. Instead of staying in the usual riding position, you take up the "forward position" (see right).

This rider is going with the horse's movement and is in the forward position.

The horse must be able to see the fence early to judge his jump.

The horse approaches the fence with rhythm, balance and impulsion.

The horse lifts his head and forelegs, while his hindlegs provide the power for the jump.

The horse should round his back over the jump.

The jump

To use the forward position, you need to know when to adopt it. The jump has five different phases, and the pictures above show you how your position should change for each one of them.

1. Approach

On the approach, you should sit deep in the saddle so you can use your seat and legs to keep your horse going. Ride straight at the middle of the fence and let your horse stretch his neck to look at it.

2. Takeoff

Lean forward slightly as you come up to the fence and, if you are using a neckstrap, take hold of it. Bend further forward as your horse takes off, so that you are in the forward position as he jumps.

Sitting in the forward position

To adopt this position, you bend forward from the hips. This moves your weight from your seat to your knees and ankles. Your lower legs should be against your horse's sides, so you can give the aids.

To balance, you need to keep your back straight and your head up.

It's easier to balance like this if you shorten your stirrups (see page 19). Take them up by about two holes, or whatever you find feels comfortable.

Begin by trying the forward position at the halt. Then practise it on the flat at the walk and trot. It may help to use a neckstrap to start with.

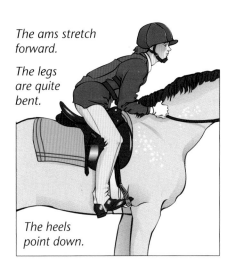

The ams stretch forward.

The legs are quite bent.

The heels point down.

To jump well, the horse needs to stretch his head forward.

The forelegs touch down one after the other, followed by the hind legs.

The horse brings his hind legs under him so he is ready to move away.

3. In the air

Stay in the forward position as your horse goes over the fence, letting your hands go forward to allow him plenty of rein. Try to look and plan ahead, so that you are ready for the landing.

4. Landing

As you land, straighten up slightly. Keep your weight in the stirrups and let your knees and ankles absorb the shock of landing. If you fall back into the saddle, you will unbalance your horse.

5. Getting away

As soon as you are back on the ground, straighten up so that you are back in your normal riding position. Take up your reins and use your seat and legs to keep your horse going.

POLEWORK

Polework, or riding over poles, is a good introduction to jumping. It regulates a horse's stride and helps improve your balance and rhythm. Polework is also a good way to learn how to approach an obstacle in a school.

Single poles

Begin with single poles spaced out around the school. Walk over them, letting your horse stretch his neck to look at them. Change your direction from time to time.

Brightly coloured poles are easier for the horse to see.

Solid, rounded poles will roll if the horse knocks them.

Once your horse is used to the poles, ride over them at a rising trot. Keep an even pace, and concentrate on your rhythm and impulsion. Don't look down, or you may lose your balance. Try this in your forward position, too.

Polework problems

• You may find it hard to keep your hands still to start with. If you do, try holding on to a neckstrap.
• If you find polework difficult at the trot, go back to walking over the poles.
• If your horse gets excited or tries to rush, ride in a circle in front of the poles to calm him down.

Approaching the poles

Always ride in a straight line over the middle of the poles. Try to relax in the saddle, and don't rush to get round. Keep turns smooth, using all the available space.

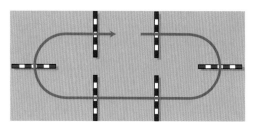

Simple route with even turns.

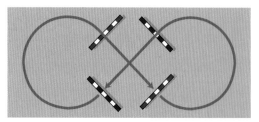

Figure of eight. Change rein in the centre.

Rows of poles

Once you can trot over single poles, try a row of three. Never use just two – your horse may think he is meant to jump them. When you can trot over three poles, add more, one at a time, until you have a row of six.

The way in which you space the poles depends on the length of your horse's stride. The table below is a rough guide.

Counting aloud over the poles may help your rhythm.

Raised poles

It is easier to keep a good line if the poles are at the edge of the school.

Place the poles like this.

Block

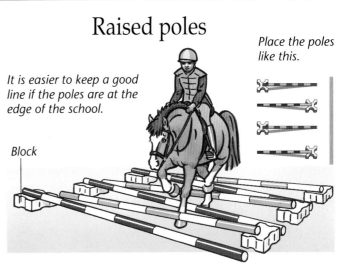

To make the exercise harder, raise the poles slightly by putting a block under alternate ends. This makes your horse take higher steps. Once you feel happy riding over raised poles in your normal position, try it in the forward position. Don't try to do too much at once, though, and end each session while your horse is going well.

Trotting pole distances

Height of horse or pony	Distance
up to 12.2hh	1.05m (3.6ft)
12.2hh - 14.2hh	1.20m (4ft)
14.2hh - 16.2hh	1.35m (4.6ft)
over 16.2hh	1.50m (5ft)

The horse steps between the poles like this.

FIRST JUMPS

The next stage after polework is to try some jumps. You should start with small, simple fences and build up your skills and confidence gradually. It is important not to overstretch your horse by trying to do too much at once.

Cross-pole fences

A low, cross-pole fence, like the one on the left, is a good first jump because the cross helps you aim for the centre. Put the fence at the side of the school, so you can use the edge to help you ride a straight approach.

Always warm up before you begin jumping. When you are ready, approach the fence at a trot. This makes it easier to control your horse and stops him getting overexcited.

A cross-pole fence looks inviting to the horse.

Placing poles

A placing pole is a pole put on the ground a small distance in front of the fence. It helps your horse judge where to take off

Placing pole

Line of approach

The pole should be placed one stride away from the fence. The length of a horse's stride varies, but the table below gives some approximate distances for a trotted approach.

Placing pole distances

Height of the horse or pony	Distance from jump
13.2hh - 14.2hh	2.15m (7ft)
14.2hh - 15.2hh	2.45m (8ft)
over 15.2hh	72.75m (9ft)

Jumping upright fences

Uprights are fences where the poles are all set directly above one another. They may look quite small but they can be hard for your horse to judge, so they require a good, straight approach.

A horse judges a fence's height from the bottom up.

You can make this easier for him by putting a pole on the ground just in front of the fence. This gives it a clear ground line.

Never try to jump a fence with the ground line pole behind it. This creates a false ground line which could confuse your horse and make him take off too late and hit the fence, or even fall.

Sloping and parallel spread fences

Sloping spreads are wide jumps which are lower at the front than at the back. They can look quite big, but the low front makes them easier. The horse can see how far he must jump, which helps him judge his takeoff.

Never approach a sloping spread from behind. If you try to jump it the wrong way, your horse will not be able to see the back rail or judge the size of the fence. A parallel spread, where the front and back are the same height, is much harder to jump.

A sloping spread helps the horse to round his back and make a good shape over the jump.

Brightly coloured poles draw the horse's attention to the fence.

COMMON FAULTS

The key to successful jumping is a good approach. Most faults begin here, affecting your position or takeoff so your horse cannot jump well. Other problems may occur if you try to do too much at once, or if your horse is afraid.

This horse was not prepared for the fence and has stopped in front of it.

When to sit forward

Sitting forward helps your horse to jump, but only if you get your timing and position right. If you sit forward either too soon or too late, you may have problems with the jump.

Sitting forward too soon

Sitting forward too late

This rider's weight has been thrown forward. This has unbalanced her horse, making it hard for him to take off.

This rider has been left behind. Unless she lets the reins slide through her fingers, she will jab her horse in the mouth.

Where to take off

As a beginner, it's best to let your horse judge the takeoff, but he may get it wrong if you don't ride a good approach. If he takes off too early or too late, he will hit the fence. A long, straight approach, a clear ground line and a placing pole all help him to judge the jump correctly.

Take off too late

Take off too early

Hitting fences

Rounded back   *Hollow back*

If your horse is hitting fences, it may help to work on your approach over trotting poles. It could also be that he is jumping with a hollow back (see above). Encourage him to round his back by trying some spreads.

Refusals

A refusal is when a horse stops dead in front of a fence. This may be because he is not prepared for it or because he finds it frightening. Try to find the cause – don't just punish him, you will only make him dislike jumping and refuse more.

Try the fence again, sitting deep in the saddle and using your legs to keep up impulsion. Don't sit forward too soon. It may help to follow another horse over.

The first horse sets a lead, giving the second horse more confidence.

Running out

This is when a horse swerves to one side at the last moment. If this happens, stop and turn him so he has to walk back past the fence. Then try it again. Don't let him avoid it.

Use firm leg aids and carry a whip on the side he runs out to. Make it harder for him to run out by building a wider fence or placing it near a wall.

Rushing

If a horse rushes at a fence, he may be eager to jump or just anxious to get it over with. Don't pull on the reins to hold him back, but circle in front of the fence until he settles.

Once your horse has stopped rushing, approach the fence at a walk. Keep the approach short and break into a trot just a few strides before takeoff.

Other problems

If you are riding well but still having problems, there may be another cause. Ask your riding instructor for help.

First, make sure your horse is not in pain. Check his tack and ask the farrier (see pages 76-77) to look at his legs and feet. Avoid jumping on hard ground.

If your horse has had a bad experience or if the fence is too big, he may be afraid. Build up his confidence over smaller fences, then try following another horse over the problem fence.

If you have tried everything without success, your horse may just be playing up. Don't let him get away with it, but reward him when he does well.

This horse is jumping two fences in a row. Jumping like this takes a lot of practice, so be patient.

COMBINATIONS

Once you can jump single fences, you may want to try a combination. This is when you jump two or more fences, one after the other. This improves your rhythm and balance, and helps you learn to judge your horse's stride.

This horse is jumping the second fence in a double.

Double and treble combinations

A combination with two fences is called a double. If it has three fences, it is called a treble. Most courses include at least one double or treble combination, so it is a good idea to practise them. You should keep the fences low to begin with. Start with a simple double, as shown below.

The next page describes how to set up different combinations. This is quite hard so, until you have lots of practice, ask an experienced person to help. You will need to know the length of your horse's stride (see right) to space the fences correctly, so your horse can take off in the right place.

Jumping a simple double combination

The horse and rider shown below are jumping a double combination of a cross pole followed by a spread. The combination has been set up to allow the horse two non-jumping strides

between the two fences. Accuracy is very important. To jump the second fence successfully, the horse needs to land in the right place after jumping the first one.

This horse and rider are jumping a simple double.

The first fence is smaller.

On landing, horse and rider prepare for the next fence.

Setting up different combinations

Start by setting up two cross-pole fences, spaced to allow your horse two non-jumping strides between them.

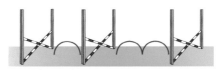

Close the distance between the fences to one stride. Then add a third fence, two strides on from the second.

Lastly, vary the type of fences. Make the last fence into an upright or a spread, and the second fence into an upright.

Measuring distances using stride lengths

To build a combination, you need to know the length of your horse's stride. Once you know what this is, you can work out how far apart the fences in a combination should be.

If you know how long your own strides are, you can measure the distances in a combination by pacing them out on the ground.

This table compares average stride lengths for a person and a 14.2hh horse.

Human strides	Horse strides	Actual distance
1	-	1m (3ft)
6-7	1	5.4-6.4m (18-21ft)
10-11	2	9-9.9m (30-33ft)

The average length of a horse's stride depends on his size – the bigger he is, the longer his stride will be. The exact length, however, varies. A horse's strides get longer when he is going faster, and shorter when he is going slowly on a hill or on soft ground. When he is jumping, his stride length will also be affected by what kind of fence he is jumping.

The horse takes off after his second stride.

The second fence is bigger.

JUMPING A COURSE

A course of fences is a real test of skill. It takes both good technique and a carefully planned route to ride round one successfully. Once you have learned to jump a course, you can take part in jumping competitions (see pages 132-133).

Walking the course

It can be hard to ride a good approach to every fence when you are jumping a whole course. However, it helps to walk round and look at the fences on foot first – even if you built them yourself.

Plan your route and then try to walk the course taking the path you intend to ride. To help you plan, you can measure the distance between fences by counting your strides as you walk round.

Walking the course helps you ride it later.

Planning a route round the course

Plan your route so that you have a straight approach to all the fences, with smooth turns in-between.

A long, straight approach will give you and your horse time to judge each fence and prepare your jump.

Imagine a line running through the middle of each fence. Aim for this centre line on your approach.

This diagram shows a simple course and how to jump it.

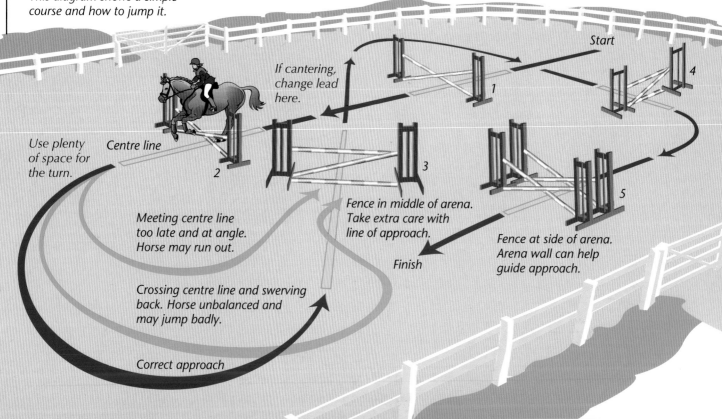

If cantering, change lead here.

Start

Use plenty of space for the turn.

Centre line

2

Meeting centre line too late and at angle. Horse may run out.

Crossing centre line and swerving back. Horse unbalanced and may jump badly.

Correct approach

1

3

Fence in middle of arena. Take extra care with line of approach.

Finish

4

5

Fence at side of arena. Arena wall can help guide approach.

Riding the course

Try to ride your planned route. Don't be tempted to cut corners and spoil your approach. Keep your head up over the jumps, so you can look and think ahead. Your horse doesn't know the route, so you need to guide him.

This rider is keeping her head up over the jump.

Approaching fences at a canter

A cantered approach gets you round more quickly and makes it easier for your horse to clear big fences. Try not to rush, though. If your horse goes too fast, he will be unbalanced and jump badly.

When cantering, your horse should strike off on his inside leg. However, he may change the lead as you go over a fence, so check before you begin the next approach.

To change the lead, go back to a trot. Then give the aids for a canter with the new lead (see pages 34-37).

If things go wrong

When you are jumping a course, your aim is to get round all the fences, so don't give up if you have a few problems on the way.

If your horse refuses or runs out, try the fence again so he learns he can't avoid it. In a competition, you must complete the course but you can have two refusals. If you knock down a fence, you are penalised but you can still complete your round.

This rider is looking ahead to the next fence. The horse is turning towards the fence and cantering with the correct leading leg for the turn.

OTHER JUMPS

If you go riding in the countryside, you may want to try jumping some natural obstacles. This is fun and good practice for cross-country, where the jumps are built out in the open.

This horse is jumping well clear of this log.

Outside the school

Jumping outside the school can be exciting, but it is important not to get carried away. Always check the jump is safe before you start and be careful how you approach it, especially if you are jumping it for the first time.

Hedges

It can be fun to jump small hedges, but always make sure the takeoff and landing are safe. You should check there is no wire in the hedge, too. Wire could injure your horse.

A horse can knock against a hedge without hurting himself, as long as there is no wire in it.

Logs

Fallen trees make good jumps as long as they don't have branches that stick out and get in the way. If you come across one, check the ground is safe on both sides before you jump it.

Ditches

Ditches make good jumps if the ground is not too muddy. If the ground is wet, the horse might slip. If the ditch is full of water, you should be especially careful when jumping it. The horse may find the water spooky, so let him take a good look at it first.

DRESSAGE

ABOUT DRESSAGE

When horses move naturally, their steps have incredible lightness, freedom and grace. Carrying a rider, however, upsets this rhythm and balance. The aim of dressage is to train a horse to regain his natural movements, and achieve harmony with his rider.

Horses naturally hold themselves gracefully.

In a dressage competition, the judges look for a well-balanced horse and rider.

Learning dressage

Dressage is simply a more advanced form of Classical riding, so horses and riders who have been taught in the Classical style will already know some of the basics.

Developing dressage skills requires specialised training and a disciplined approach. The horse learns to respond to the slightest movement from his rider, and the rider learns to give the aids very precisely. This work begins quite simply, however, by trying to improve movements that are already familiar – for example, transitions from one pace to another, turns and circles.

Different stages

There are six different levels of dressage that you can aim for. They are Preliminary, Novice, Elementary, Medium, Advanced Medium and Advanced. There are new, more difficult movements to learn and perform at each level, and there are competitions you can enter at these levels as well. Dressage competitions are called tests. The tests are described on pages 134-135.

What you need

For basic dressage, you can use a general purpose saddle and a simple snaffle bridle. If you hope to compete regularly, you may want to start using a dressage saddle. This has straighter flaps than a general purpose saddle, allowing the rider's legs to lie closer to the horse's sides. It also helps to use a dressage whip. This is longer than a standard whip, so you don't need to take your hands off the reins to use it.

Snaffle bridle (see page 14)

Dressage saddle

Dressage whip

This picture shows the straight cut of a dressage saddle.

The dressage seat

The rider sits upright with her back straight.

Longer stirrups make the rider's legs straighter.

The dressage seat is similar to the classical seat. You sit deep in the saddle with your back straight. Your arms form a line from the elbow, down the reins to the horse's mouth. The main difference, as you improve, is that you ride with your stirrups about two holes longer. This makes your legs straighter, giving you more contact with your horse's sides.

Dressage at Advanced level

Advanced dressage riders use a double bridle and wear spurs. A double bridle has two sets of reins and two bits, which give the rider a lot of control. The spurs are used to give very precise aids.

Spurs can be worn at any level, though you may need to ask for permission in Pony Club tests. You can't use a double bridle at Preliminary or Novice level, but it is compulsory for Advanced riders.

This rider is performing an Advanced dressage test.

The horse is wearing a double bridle, and the rider is wearing spurs.

GOING WELL

The way a horse is working and his obedience to the aids is called his "way of going". If he is balanced, moving freely and in tune with his rider, he is "going well". One of the aims of dressage is to achieve this as much as possible.

This horse and rider are balanced and working well together.

Accepting the bit

When a horse responds well to the messages he receives from your hands, and holds the bit in his mouth without fighting it, he is "accepting the bit" or "on the bit". His neck should be arched in a smooth curve, and his head should be held vertical without looking tense or stiff.

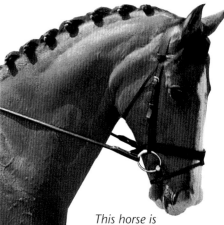

This horse is accepting the bit.

Engaging the hocks

Here, you can see the powerful action of the horse's hocks.

Most of your horse's power is in his hindquarters. To use this energy properly, his hind legs need to be tucked under his body and working hard, not trailing out behind him. Doing this correctly is called "engaging the hocks".

A rounded outline

When a horse is on the bit and engaging his hocks, his body looks compact and rounded. He is said to have a "rounded outline".

In order to achieve a rounded outline, as shown here, you have to do a lot of work on your horse's balance, rhythm and impulsion.

Impulsion

Impulsion is the energy in a horse's stride. However, it is more than just speed, or liveliness. It is energy and power which are under control, and which the horse can channel into different movements when he is asked to. A horse can move very slowly, but with plenty of impulsion.

To create more impulsion, you need to use your legs to ask for more energy, and use your seat and hands to control it.

This horse is demonstrating good impulsion, balance and rhythm.

Balance

When a horse is unbalanced he carries his weight over his forelegs or "on the forehand". As his balance improves, he brings his hind legs under him, engaging his hocks. Riding up hills is a good way to work on this.

His hind legs are pushing him along powerfully.

Rhythm

Ideally, a horse should be able to keep a steady rhythm in each pace. If he is unbalanced, he may start to rush and lose the rhythm of his stride. You can prevent this by building up his work gradually.

His neck is arched, and his head is close to the vertical.

Behind the bit

If you pull too hard on the reins, your horse may start to resist by going "behind the bit". This is when he tucks his head in towards his chest to avoid the pressure from the bit.

When a horse's head is tucked back like this, he is said to be "over-bending". The best way to prevent him from doing this is to relax your hands as soon as he obeys your hand aids.

This horse has tucked his head in towards his chest. This means that his neck and jaw are tense.

A hollow outline

When a horse resists his rider, he tends to poke his nose out and hollow his back instead of working with a rounded outline. This shows that he is unbalanced. Work on making your seat secure and your aids clear and firm.

LINES AND CIRCLES

A well-balanced horse is able to control his movements precisely. He can do difficult things such as move in a perfectly straight line or in a tight circle. However, this takes practice and has to be learned gradually. It's very important that his rider is balanced, too.

This horse and rider are balancing well as they circle.

Better turns and circles

Working on circles is important for developing a horse's suppleness and balance. With practice, the muscles around his spine become more supple, so that he is able to make tighter turns without "falling out" or "falling in" (see below). Once his balance, rhythm and impulsion begin to improve, you will find circles easier.

Falling in, falling out

When a horse's spine is not curved around the shape of the circle, he is said to be falling in or falling out, depending on which part of his body isn't bending properly, or is bending too much. These are the most common problems and what causes them:

Here, the rider is using too much inside rein, so the horse's outside shoulder and neck are falling out.

Here, the rider is not using enough outside leg behind the girth, so the horse's outside hindquarters are falling out.

This rider is using too little inside leg at the same time as pulling too hard on the inside rein, so the horse's inside shoulder is falling in.

Keeping straight

Riding in a straight line is not as easy as it sounds. Horses don't naturally move in straight lines, and they find it even harder when carrying a rider. It is, however, one of the things that you are asked to show in all levels of dressage tests.

If you find it difficult to keep straight, check how your weight is distributed in the saddle. You may be sitting crookedly and throwing your horse off balance. It's also possible that you are riding with one rein slightly longer than the other.

This horse is crooked, because his rider is slumped slightly to the left.

This horse and rider are straight.

Tracking up

When a horse trots, he "tracks up", which means his hind feet land in the tracks of his fore feet. At walk and in extended paces, his hindlegs overtrack, or step over the tracks of his forelegs, but they should still land right behind each other. Check your horse's tracks to see if he is moving straight.

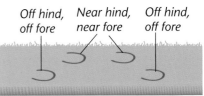

Off hind, off fore *Near hind, near fore* *Off hind, off fore*

Tracking up at trot.

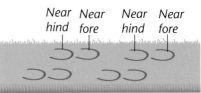

Near hind *Near fore* *Near hind* *Near fore*

Overtracking at extended trot.

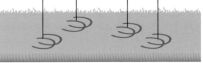

Hind hooves to one side of fore hooves.

Tracks showing that the horse is crooked.

Walking backwards, or reining back

Reining back means asking a horse to walk backwards in a straight line. It's easiest to ask him to do this alongside something straight, such as the side of the school. Place both your legs behind the girth and squeeze. If he tries to move forward, resist his movement gently with the reins using a give-and-take action. Never try to yank him back with the reins as this will make him stiffen up.

This horse is reining back correctly, although he is showing some resistance.

TRANSITIONS

This horse is moving from trot to canter.

Working on transitions between the paces, for example from walk to trot, forms an important part of dressage training. A horse should be able to move from one pace to another smoothly, without losing his balance and impulsion.

Why practise transitions?

When you ask your horse to change pace, he has to do two things: he has to understand and obey your instructions, and he has to use the correct muscles to carry out the transition smoothly. So, the more you work on transitions, the more obedient, supple and balanced he is likely to become. Working on transitions also helps him develop the ability to shorten and lengthen his strides, called "collection" and "extension" (see pages 120-121).

Using the half-halt

A half-halt is when you ask a horse to check slightly without changing pace. To do this, sit deep in the saddle and increase the contact on the reins, then quickly push him on again. This makes him pay attention and increase his impulsion, so it is useful to use before a transition.

This rider is asking for a half-halt.

Upward transitions

This horse is moving from walk to trot.

Upward transitions are moves from a slower pace to a faster one – halt to walk, walk to trot and trot to canter. With enough practice, you will be able to ask for upward transitions with very light aids that appear almost invisible to people watching.

Downward transitions

Although slowing down may seem easy, it is more difficult for your horse make smooth downward transitions. Bracing your lower back and seat muscles will tell him to slow from one pace to another, but he shouldn't lose impulsion and balance as he changes pace. He should also remain on the bit. It helps to use a half-halt before you ask for the transition, so that he is concentrating on slowing down. As with upward transitions, the more you practise, the more subtle your aids will become.

This horse is slowing down smoothly from canter to trot.

Walk to canter, canter to walk

As your transitions improve and your horse becomes more responsive, you can learn to move straight from walk to canter, and vice versa. This demonstrates that your horse is balanced and on the bit, and that he is moving with plenty of impulsion.

Walk to canter

A steady canter

Canter to walk

This horse and rider are moving smoothly from walk to canter and back again.

1. For walk to canter, make sure your horse is walking with plenty of impulsion. Give the aids for canter firmly and clearly so that he knows you are not asking for trot.

2. For canter to walk, first continue to trot for a few strides in between canter and walk. Do this until you and your horse are completely confident about the transition.

3. Gradually give less and less time to trotting in between canter and walk. Your horse will need to be very balanced before he can control these downward transitions easily.

WORKING ON PACES

Once a horse's balance and impulsion have begun to improve, he can vary the length of his strides when his rider asks him to. He can make them shorter, which is called "collecting", or he can make them longer, called "extending".

Collection and extension

When a horse collects or extends, the rhythm of his stride stays the same – he simply takes bigger or smaller steps. When he collects, he takes shorter strides which cover less ground; when he extends, his strides are longer and he covers more ground.

It's very difficult for a horse to learn collection or extension, so he should only be taught very gradually. If he's rushed, he may become unbalanced and start to resist. Teaching starts in trot, as it is easiest for the horse to stay balanced in this pace.

In trot, the basic pace is called working trot. If the strides are shorter, it is called collected trot. If the strides are slightly longer, it is called medium trot. At full stretch, it is called extended trot. There is the same range of collection and extension in canter.

This horse is demonstrating working trot.

Here, the strides are shorter, showing collected trot.

At medium trot, the horse stretches his strides slightly.

Here, the horse is working towards a full extended trot.

Working at walk

The basic walk is called the medium walk. Collected and extended walk also exist, but they are difficult to achieve. There is something called the free walk as well. This is when the horse relaxes and stretches out his neck muscles without losing balance or impulsion.

A good, balanced free walk

Transitions

When a horse moves from one level of collection or extension to another – for example, from medium trot to extended trot – this is called a transition even though he doesn't change pace. At first, however, you don't work on complete transitions, as the increase or decrease in your horse's length of stride is quite small.

Starting to collect

This horse is beginning to show some collection, but needs a little more impulsion.

Before asking for collection, work in sitting trot until your horse is balanced and going well. Then, use a half-halt to gain his full attention and increase his impulsion.

Maintain his impulsion by keeping your legs next to his sides, but restrain his forward movement gently with your seat and hands. He should shorten his strides slightly.

When he has shortened his steps for four or five strides, release the resistance in your hands. Send him back into working trot, letting him lengthen his strides again.

Starting to extend

It's best to start extension work in rising trot. When your horse is moving at a balanced working trot, let him extend his neck out a little further by moving your hands up his neck. Don't loosen the reins as this may cause him to lose balance.

As he stretches out his neck, help him to maintain the impulsion he needs by squeezing with your legs on the girth. He should then lengthen his strides slightly, too. After lengthening for a few strides, bring him back into working trot again.

The next stage

Once your horse shortens or lengthens his stride when asked, you can ask him to do so for longer periods, but never for too long. Gradually, ask him to shorten his stride further for a true collected trot, or extend it into medium and extended trot. You can also start to extend and collect in canter.

Working at collected canter

LATERAL WORK

Lateral work is when a horse moves sideways as well as forwards. There are many different lateral movements, and they vary widely in difficulty. Once your horse accepts your aids and you can get him balanced, he is ready to start learning some of the simpler ones.

Lateral aids

For all the basic lateral movements, you use mainly your inside leg and outside rein. The key is to use these aids at the same time, co-ordinating them, so that the horse understands that he has to move sideways.

The inside leg, used firmly on the girth, asks for sideways movement. Move it back slightly if your horse doesn't respond. Contact on the outside rein controls the forward movement.

Your outside leg and inside rein are hardly used at all, although in some movements (such as shoulder-in) you use them slightly more.

This horse is moving sideways across the school using a movement called leg yielding (see opposite page).

Learning to turn on the forehand

To perform a turn on the forehand, a horse moves his hindlegs around his forelegs, which stay on one spot. It is not required in dressage tests, but it is a useful move to learn, as it can help you with opening gates. When you first learn this, only ask your horse to move a few steps at a time.

A turn on the forehand can be performed from walk, but start at halt at first. Use your inside leg firmly on the girth, or slightly behind it. Your outside leg just rests behind the girth. Keep a firm contact on your outside rein to stop him moving forward. With your inside rein, turn his head slightly to encourage a bend to the inside.

The horse's forelegs mark time on the spot.

122

How to begin leg yielding

In leg yield, a horse moves sideways and forwards with his body and neck straight, and his head flexed at the poll, slightly away from the direction he's moving. It's easiest to ask for this in walk. He is already moving forward, so you just need to ask him to move sideways as well.

It's best to walk down the 5m line of the school, then leg yield into the outside track.

For leg yield to the left, squeeze firmly with your right leg on or slightly behind the girth to ask for the sideways movement. Use contact on your outside rein to control the forward movement. Use the leg and hand aid together so that he moves forwards and sideways smoothly.

You may need to keep him moving forward with a slight outside leg aid. You can also use your right rein very lightly to bend his head to the right.

You can see that the horse's off foreleg is moving sideways.

Working on shoulder-in

Shoulder-in is when a horse moves forward down the track, but with his shoulder bent away from the direction he's moving in. In this position, he makes three sets of tracks instead of two. Ask for shoulder-in at walk at first, then in trot. It helps to ride a 10m circle in the corner of the school before asking for shoulder-in, as this positions the horse correctly.

This diagram shows how the horse makes three tracks with his feet.

You should look straight down the track as you move

It may help to turn your shoulders inwards slightly.

As the circle brings you level with the side of the school, give a half-halt with your outside rein. Squeeze with your inside leg on the girth. Use your outside leg slightly to stop his hindquarters from falling out of line, and your inside rein gently to ask him to bend his neck to the inside.

Ideally, your horse should move down the school with his shoulder at 30° from the edge. The horse in the picture is at a bigger angle than this.

THE NEXT STAGE

As a horse's balance, obedience and collection improve, he is able to perform dressage moves of greater and greater difficulty. However, even at advanced stages, he should still be taught very gradually.

This horse and rider are working at a balanced counter canter.

Counter canter

Counter canter means deliberately cantering with the outside leg at canter, instead of the inside leg. Horses naturally canter on the inside leg, so performing counter canter demonstrates their balance and obedience to the aids.

Demi-pirouettes

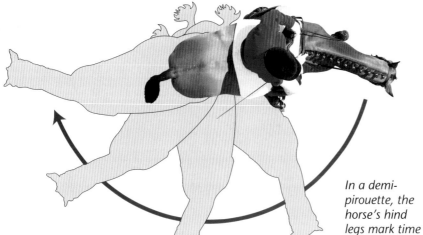

In a demi-pirouette, the horse's hind legs mark time on the spot.

Once you can perform a turn on the forehand without too much trouble, you can learn the demi-pirouette in walk. This is like the turn on the forehand, but the aids are different and the hind legs stay on one spot instead of the forelegs. It is harder for a horse to do this.

Travers and half-pass

Travers and half-pass are more lateral moves. In these, the horse's neck is bent slightly towards the direction of the movement.

In travers, the horse's forelegs and shoulders move on the outside track. His hindquarters move on the inside track, at an angle of about 30° from the edge of the school.

Half-pass is similar to travers, but the horse moves across the school instead of along its edge. This makes it harder to control the move properly.

COMPETITIONS

GOING TO COMPETITIONS

There are many kinds of riding competitions, but all require careful planning. You need to know what to take and how to travel, and what to do when you get there.

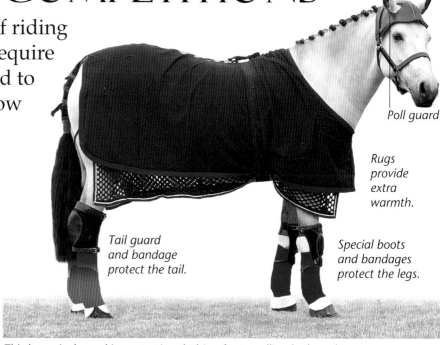

Poll guard

Rugs provide extra warmth.

Tail guard and bandage protect the tail.

Special boots and bandages protect the legs.

This horse is dressed in protective clothing for travelling by horsebox.

What to take

You will need different things for each kind of competition. There may be special rules on dress or presentation, so check beforehand and make sure you have everything you need.

Checklist:
- ✓ Tack, including spares
- ✓ Protective boots/bandages
- ✓ Headcollar, lead rope, rugs
- ✓ Money for entry fees/phone
- ✓ Grooming and first aid kits
- ✓ Haynet, bucket and water
- ✓ Riding clothes

Travelling to a competition

You may be able to hack to a local competition, if it is not too far away. Plan your route so you have plenty of time and don't need to hurry. Take what you need in a backpack, or arrange for someone to bring your things by car.

If the competition is further afield, you may need to take your horse in a trailer or horsebox. Some horses don't like travelling like this, so it's a good idea to practise before the day of the competition so your horse can get used to it.

Loading a horse into a trailer

First, line the trailer with straw to stop the horse slipping. Hang up a haynet too, for him to eat on the way.

Lead the horse slowly and calmly up the ramp into the trailer. Let him stop to look at the ramp if he wants.

Once inside, tie him up fairly short. Leave the trailer by the "jockey" door in the side and shut it behind you.

An experienced person should raise the ramp and check everything is secure before you set off.

On the way

If you are going to a local show, you probably won't need to stop on the way. On a longer journey, just take a half-way break. Never enter a horsebox or trailer while it is moving.

Arriving

Try to arrive early, so you have time to smarten up and warm up before you compete. If you hacked to the competition, dismount and unsaddle when you arrive. If you travelled by horsebox or trailer, unload and walk your horse around so he can stretch. Don't leave your horse, tack or equipment unattended.

This rider has tied her horse to the side of the horsebox. In bad weather, however, it may be better to leave horses inside.

Settling your horse and getting ready

Tie up your horse in a sheltered spot and, if there is time, give him a small haynet. Offer him water from his own bucket. Don't share buckets or let him touch muzzles with strange horses, to avoid risk of infection.

Once you have settled your horse, you should go to the Secretary's tent to find out when you are competing and where you need to go. You may be given a number to wear while you compete.

Leave someone experienced to look after your horse while you are gone. If you have friends at the show, it is a good idea to tie up your horses near each other, so you can take it in turns to keep an eye on them.

Make sure you are ready in good time. When it is nearly time for you to start, go into the collecting ring. This is where you wait for your turn in the arena.

Competitions can be unsettling for a horse, so it's important to reassure him.

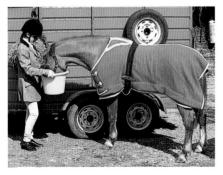

If it is cold, a horse should wear a rug while waiting.

GYMKHANAS

Gymkhanas are competitions involving different mounted games. They are often held as part of larger shows which include other events such as jumping. Most people take part in gymkhana games for fun, but they also help develop riding skills. Success requires accuracy, speed and a good rapport with your pony. Games and rules vary between competitions, but this page shows some of the most popular ones.

These riders are competing in a "Pony Club" race. In this game, you race to collect and hang up letters, spelling out "PONY CLUB".

Stepping stones

In this game, you race to a row of "stepping stones", dismount and run along them. You then ride to the finish.

Sack race

In a sack race, you ride to your sack, dismount and get into it. You then lead your pony to the finish by shuffling along.

Ball and bucket

In this game, you collect balls and drop them into a bucket. When you have got all the balls, you race to the finish.

Practising

The main key to success in gymkhana games is practice. Both pony and rider must be fit and know what they are meant to do. If a game involves special equipment, the pony must be used to it or he may spook.

Team games

In some competitions, riders compete in teams. Most Pony Clubs and some riding schools have a games team, and joining one is a good way to learn more about mounted games. The regular training sessions help you keep fit, too.

These gymkhana ponies need to be calm, confident and obedient. To do well in team games, they must also enjoy being with other ponies.

Flying dismounts and vaulting

In most gymkhana games, you can save time if you can dismount while your pony is moving. This is called a flying dismount. It's useful to be able to do this to either side.

Some riders also learn to mount while their ponies are moving. This is called vaulting. It is quite hard to do, but it is much quicker than mounting the usual way.

Neck reining

Carrying equipment in games is easier if you know how to neck rein, Western-style (see pages 58-59). With Classical tack, however, you should shorten your reins first.

A flying dismount

Push out as you dismount.

As you land, start running.

Shortening and holding the reins

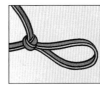

Knot the reins just above the pony's withers.

Hold the knot in one hand, keeping your palm down.

WESTERN SHOWS

A Western show is divided into different categories, or "classes", for different kinds of horse. Mounted games are often held, too. There are many Western shows in the United States. Elsewhere, Western riding associations may organize shows or provide information about them (see page 144).

This horse and rider are dressed for a show.

Western show classes

Western show classes are designed to test the ability of both horse and rider. Competitors can take part in Western riding, pleasure or trail classes.

A Western riding horse should be a good all-round horse. This class tests his manners and how he moves. His rider's position and use of the aids are also judged.

A "pleasure" horse should be a pleasure to ride. He is shown at the walk, jog and lope. He is judged on his manners, performance and appearance, as well as how suitable he is for his rider.

A trail horse is judged on his behaviour and skills. He must be calm and obedient, and move well at the walk, jog and lope. He may have to negotiate natural obstacles or carry awkward objects, too.

The rider on the left is taking part in a pleasure class. In this class, the horse must show complete obedience to the aids.

Mounted games

Many different games are played in Western competitions. Some are similar to gymkhana games (see pages 128-129), but others are specifically designed to test Western skills such as neck reining. Barrel racing is one of the most popular games, along with flag and keyhole races.

Reining pattern

This horse is doing a sliding stop.

The reining pattern class is the Western equivalent of a dressage test (see pages 134-135). The horse performs set movements, including dramatic stops and turns, transitions and changes of lead.

Keyhole race

In this game, a keyhole shape is marked on the ground in flour. During the race, the horse should not step outside the keyhole. If he does, his feet kick up a cloud of flour.

When the race begins you ride down the keyhole, stop and turn in the circle at the top, and then race back to the start.

Barrel racing

For this game, three barrels are set up in the arena. You race around the barrels and back to the finish, following a set route. This requires skill as well as speed – the tighter the turns, the faster you can complete the race.

In a barrel race, you ride around the barrels in a cloverleaf pattern.

Flag race

In a flag race, the aim is to collect several flags and drop them in a container without dismounting. In an individual event, you collect all the flags yourself, one at a time. In a team competition, each member of the team collects one flag.

SHOW JUMPING

Jumping competitions are a great test of skill for both horse and rider. Any rider who can jump a course (see pages 108-109) should be able to find a competition to suit them. You can also learn a lot from watching a competition, whether on television or at a show.

Competition jumps

Show jumps are similar to the kind of fences you might set up yourself. They are brightly coloured and they fall down easily if a horse knocks them. The jumps are set up differently for each category or "class" in a competition. Competitors must jump all the jumps in the correct order, though they can plan their own routes around the course. A longer route may be easier, but a shorter one can save valuable seconds. Penalties are given for faults (see right).

Beginners' classes

Classes are usually divided according to age, experience, or the height of your horse. There will probably be several beginners' classes at a local show.

Minimus classes are excellent for beginners. You can only enter these if you and your horse have not won anything before. Clear-round classes are also a good place to start. Here, you ride the course just once. You win a rosette if you jump "clear", with no faults.

Accuracy is more important than speed in a clear-round class.

Other classes

More experienced riders usually enter either Novice or Intermediate classes. An Open Class is the most difficult class to compete in. It has no restrictions on entry at all, so very experienced riders may take part.

For the more advanced classes, the jumps are made bigger. They are also built in more difficult combinations, so competitors need to plan their routes carefully and ride with great accuracy.

Competition rules and penalties

Most competitions are divided into two rounds. In the first round, the aim is to jump clear. Any faults, such as refusals, are penalised.

Competitors who succeed in the first round go into a second, called a jump-off. In this round, there are fewer fences, but they are bigger. The competitors are timed, too. Whoever has the fastest round with no faults wins.

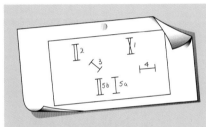

The course plan shows the order in which you must tackle the jumps.

You can take the fence again if your horse refuses.

Penalties, called faults, are awarded as follows:
• 3 faults for the first refusal or run-out, or for circling in front of a fence;
• 4 faults for knocking down a fence;
• 6 faults for a second refusal.

Competitors are eliminated for a third refusal, falling off, taking the wrong course, starting before the bell or failing to pass through the start or finish.

Equitation jumping

In Equitation jumping, you are judged on style as well as penalties, so it is good practice for your technique.

This rider is going with the horse's movement.

This horse has tucked up his front legs in order to clear this parallel spread.

A parallel spread is difficult to jump because the front pole is as high as the back one.

DRESSAGE

A dressage competition is called a test. The aim of the test is to show how well a horse and rider understand each other, as well as how skillful they are. Tests only last about five minutes, but they are very demanding. It takes months of practice to prepare for one.

Competing

Dressage competitions are divided into six levels. Beginners usually start with Preliminary tests. These are followed by Novice, Elementary, Medium, Advanced Medium and Advanced level tests.

Local riding schools and Pony Clubs usually have details of competitions. Entering one is a good way to see how your training is going. It can also be helpful to watch other riders.

In a competition test, you perform a set sequence of movements. These vary from test to test, but you can check what will be included by writing to the organisers.

Turn out

Both horse and rider need to be smartly turned out for a test. Their clothes and tack must conform to competition rules, and the horse should be thoroughly groomed.

Scoring

At the end of a test, competitors are given a scoresheet with the judge's comments. Each movement is marked from 0 (not performed) to 10 (excellent). There are also marks for the judge's general impression.

This horse and rider are taking part in a Preliminary test.

Advanced Dressage Competitions

Riders competing at an advanced level use dressage saddles and double bridles to give them better control. Their horses have reached a high level of obedience and collection (see pages 116-117). They perform very difficult movements, some of which are shown below.

This competitor is performing a demi-pirouette in canter.

The horse canters a half-circle without moving forward or backward.

Piaffe

Piaffe is a light, springy movement.

Piaffe is like trotting on the spot. The horse springs from one pair of legs to the other, with a clear moment of suspension between steps.

Passage

Passage is a smooth movement.

Passage is a slow, high - stepping trot. There is a long moment of suspension, when it seems like the horse is moving in slow motion.

Flying Change

A flying change demands split second timing.

In a flying change, the horse changes his leading leg in canter, during the moment of suspension, rather than going back to walk or trot.

CROSS-COUNTRY

This horse and rider are tackling a cross-country jump.

A cross-country competition takes place in the open. Competitors ride across fields, through woods, over hills and down tracks, tackling all kinds of natural fences and obstacles on the way.

Different fences

These are some of the more common fences.

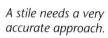
A stile needs a very accurate approach.

A stone wall has a clear ground line.

A tiger trap may be built over a ditch.

A bullfinch has a soft, brush top.

Parallel bars are difficult to judge.

A drop fence is lower on the landing side.

Cross-country courses

In cross-country competitions, the fences are spread out over a much bigger distance than in show jumping. The course can cover several fields, so you probably won't be able to see all the fences at once. The fences are made of natural materials and can be built on all kinds of ground, including difficult slopes and drops. They are usually solidly built, so they don't fall down when they are knocked. This means that they should only be tackled by experienced horses and riders.

These riders are competing together in a pairs class. The first rider is setting a lead, encouraging the second horse to follow over the jump.

Different ground

A course can cover all kinds of ground. If it is hilly, riders must be careful not to go too fast and tire their horses. They will also try to avoid very muddy or hard ground, which could hurt their horses' legs. Many jumps are set on slopes, requiring a careful approach.

This horse is making a powerful jump out of the water.

Other events

Cross-country forms an important part of three-day events (see pages 138-139), along with show jumping and dressage. There are also non-competitive cross-country events. The non-competitive events usually have shorter courses and easier jumps, so they are ideal for riders with less experience.

A fallen log like this makes a nice, solid jump, so it is a good introduction to cross-country fences.

Planning a route

Before the competition begins, the riders walk the course and plan their routes. Competitors may take very different approaches to the same fence, as this diagram shows.

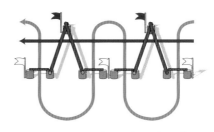

Competitors must keep the white flags on their left and the red flags on their right.

There are two ways of tackling the combination shown above. The longer route (in blue) is much easier than the shorter route (in red). Competitors may, however, be able to save time if they can manage the more difficult route.

This rider is saving time by jumping this hedge close to one corner.

THREE-DAY EVENTS

A three-day event includes dressage, cross-country and show jumping, so it is really three competitions in one. A different contest is held on each day, so competitors need all-round skill as well as stamina. One-day events with similar contests are also popular.

This horse and rider are taking part in a dressage test on the first day of a three-day event.

At the event

On day one, competitors take part in a dressage test. This is followed by a speed and endurance test, including a cross-country section, on day two. Show jumping is held on the last day.

This horse and rider are about to compete in a dressage test, which requires a smart turnout.

Bandages are not allowed during the test, so a helper is removing them.

Day one

For the dressage test, competitors must complete a set sequence of different dressage movements. These are judged on style and obedience, and marked out of ten. Each competitor's score is then converted into penalty points. The better a competitor has done, the lower his or her score will be.

When the dressage is over, competitors start preparing for day two. They walk the cross-country course and plan their route. They also work out how fast to ride the different sections, so they don't overtire their horses.

Day two

The second day is divided into four sections designed to test the competitors' stamina. First, they must cover a set distance in a section called roads and tracks, which is ridden fairly slowly. Next comes the steeplechase, where they race over a series of soft, brush fences.

This is followed by more roads and tracks. Finally, the competitors ride over a cross-country course. They must jump clear over all the fences, within a set time, to avoid penalties. The fences often include spectacular water jumps and drop fences, so it can be very exciting to watch.

Jumping out of water slows a horse down, so he needs good impulsion to make a jump like this.

Day three

Show jumps like this one test the precision of horse and rider.

The show jumping section is a test of fitness as well as accuracy and ability. The jumps are not usually very difficult, but it can be hard for a tired horse and rider to complete the course without any penalties.

At the end of the event, the scores for all three days are added together. Whoever has the lowest score (the fewest penalties) is the winner.

Shorter events

Although most top-level events take place over three days, one and two day events are also held. At Pony and Riding Club level, events last one day. For riders who have not competed in an event before, these shorter events are a good way to practise and gain experience.

A show is a chance to see different horses.

SHOWING

In a showing competition, the horses are judged on how well they move, behave and look. Competitions are divided into categories, called classes, for horses of different types, sizes and ages. They are good places to watch quality horses and to learn about breeds.

At a show

There are different classes for all kinds of horses and ponies, from Thoroughbred horses to family ponies. Most shows have separate horse and pony classes.

The judge looks carefully at each horse or pony.

Showing classes like this one require a smart appearance. The horses' manes have been plaited and the riders are wearing jackets and ties.

Family pony

The family pony class is popular with beginners. The pony should be a good all-rounder and suitable for more than one member of a family. He will be judged on how well he performs when ridden, rather than on looks.

Tack and turnout

A "tack and turnout" class is a good place for a new rider to start. This class is judged on "turnout" or presentation – the horse or pony must be well groomed and his tack must be spotless. His rider should look smart, too.

Show and riding

This class is for finely bred horses and ponies, often part or full Thoroughbreds.

This show and riding pony has typically refined features and a delicate build.

The class begins with everyone riding together. Next, each rider goes through the paces (walk, trot and canter) on their own. In a horse class, the judge rides the horses. Lastly, the judge inspects each horse or pony.

Show hunter class

This class is for sturdier horses and ponies than those in the show and riding class. A show hunter should be strong enough to gallop across country all day, as he would if he were hunting. Show hunters are shown in a similar way to the show and riding horses and ponies, except that they are also ridden at the gallop.

This rider has removed her pony's saddle for the judge's final inspection.

This is a show hunter pony. Show hunters have quite refined features, but they are also strong.

Working hunter horses and ponies

Working hunters have a heavier build and less refined features than show hunters. They are judged on how well they jump as well as on their build and appearance.

Working hunters have to jump a course of rustic-style fences.

This working hunter is correctly turned out, with plain, practical tack.

The jumping section is held first. Competitors who jump a clear round go on to put their hunters through their paces in a group. Horses are then ridden by the judge, while ponies are shown individually by their riders. Lastly, the horses or ponies are led out one at a time for the judge to inspect. This is called running up in-hand.

GLOSSARY

There are quite a lot of specialised terms to do with riding and pony care. This glossary explains some of the common terms used in this book. Words which appear in italics are defined elsewhere in the glossary.

aids – the signals a rider gives a horse to tell him what to do. Signals given with the rider's hands, seat and legs are called natural aids. Whips and spurs are called artificial aids.

breed – a particular kind of horse or pony. If a horse's parents both belong to the same breed, he is said to be purebred. If they belong to different breeds, he is said to be crossbred.

Classical riding – riding European-style, with short stirrups and both hands on the reins.

collection – when a horse shortens the length of his strides without altering his rhythm.

diagonals – the diagonal pairs of legs which move together as a horse trots. In *rising trot*, the rider is said to rise on the left or right diagonal.

disunited canter – an unbalanced canter, which has a different sequence of footfalls from a normal canter.

dressage – a form of riding where a horse performs set *movements* in response to precise *aids*.

extension – when a horse increases the length of his strides without altering his rhythm.

farrier – someone who looks after horses' feet, trimming their hooves and fitting shoes.

forward position – how a rider sits for jumping, leaning forward to take the weight off a horse's back.

gymkhana – a riding competition with games.

hacking – riding out in the open.

half-halt – when a rider checks a horse slightly without changing pace, in order to gain his attention.

hands – a unit of measurement used to measure a horse's height. One hand equals exactly 4 inches, which is about 10 cm.

horse – a general word for a horse or a *pony*.

impulsion - the energy in a horse's strides.

inside – the side that is on the inside of the curved path a horse takes when turning or circling.

lateral movements – sideways movements.

leading leg – the foreleg that stretches further forward than the other when a horse canters. A horse can lead with either foreleg, but on a bend he should lead with his *inside* leg.

left rein – the rein on the left side of a horse. Riding on the left rein means turning or circling to the left, in an anti-clockwise direction.

lunging – when a horse is exercised in a circle on a long rein, called a lunge rein, which is held by someone standing on the ground.

martingale – a leather strap that is attached to the bridle to stop a horse from throwing his head up.

movement – in *dressage*, a movement is what a rider asks a horse to do, such as a *transition*, turn or circle.

napping – when a horse won't go forward or obey his rider's *aids*.

near side – a horse's left side.

neck reining – how a rider turns a horse, *Western*-style, by laying the reins across the horse's neck.

numnah – a pad that goes under a saddle.

off side – a horse's right side.

outside – the side that is on the outside of the curved path a horse takes when turning or circling.

paces – the different ways a horse moves. There are four paces. In *Classical riding*, these are called walk, trot, canter and gallop. In *Western riding*, the trot is called the jog and the canter is called the lope.

picking out – cleaning a horse's feet.

points – the different parts of a horse's body.

pony – a *horse* that stands 14.2 *hands* high or less at the shoulder may be called a pony.

quartering – a quick groom.

right rein – the rein on the right side of a horse. Riding on the right rein means turning or circling to the right, in a clockwise direction.

rising trot – when a rider rises out of the saddle in time to the horse's movement at trot.

school – an enclosed space where riders can practise their riding skills.

seat – the way a rider sits and uses his or her weight in the saddle.

sitting trot – when a rider stays sitting in the saddle while a horse trots.

skepping out – removing droppings from a stable.

snaffle – a popular kind of bit. There are several types of snaffle; most are quite gentle on the horse's mouth.

spooking – when a horse is startled by something or shies away from it.

tack – a general word for the saddle and bridle.

transition – a change of *pace*. In *dressage*, a change in the level of *collection* or *extension* in a horse's strides may also be called a transition.

turnout – the presentation and appearance of a horse and his rider, including clothes, *tack* and grooming.

Western riding – riding American-style, with long stirrups and the reins held in one hand.

INDEX

USEFUL ADDRESSES

If you want information about where to ride, where competitions are taking place or if you want to find out about current safety standards, these organisations may be able to help you.

The British Horse Society
Stoneleigh Deer Park
Kenilworth
Warwickshire CV8 2XZ
UK
Tel: 08701 202 244
Fax: 01926 707 800

United States Pony Clubs, Inc.
4071 Iron Works Parkway
Lexington, KY
40511 - 8462
USA
Tel: 859-254-7669
Fax: 859-233-4652

Canadian Pony Club
C.P.C. National Office
Box 127
Baldur, Manitoba
R0K 0B0
Tel: 1-888-286-PONY
Fax: 1-204-535-2289

The Pony Club
Stoneleigh Park
Kenilworth
Warwickshire CV8 2RW
UK
Tel: 02476 698300
Fax: 02476 696836

Certified Horsemanship Association
5318 Old Bullard Rd
Tyler TX 75703
USA
Tel: (800) 399-0138

New Zealand Pony Clubs Association Inc.
P.O. Box 8626
Havelock North
New Zealand 4230
Tel and Fax: 0064 6 873 5464

Western Horsemen's Association of Great Britain
Brookglen,Brook Lane
Brookville
Thetford
Norfolk IP26 4RG
UK

Pony Club Australia
PO Box 46
Lockhart
New South Wales
Australia 2656
Tel: 61 07 36660446
Fax: 61 07 36660785

With thanks to Anna Claybourne

With thanks to models Katie Birch on Jake, Alison Higgins on Jessica, Carly Alder on Bobby's Girl, Kate Furzer on Honey, Terri Perry on Wellie and Max, Danielle Reddan on Alfie, Zoe Reddan on Styllo, Philippa Reed on Lucy and Solly, Ciara Gourley on Fionnula, Brook and Carly, Victoria Moore on Sonny, Ricky Cooper and Copperfield's Nutmeg, Victoria Barry on CJ, Alison Berman on Squirrel Nutkin, Nicola Ridley on Happy and Amy Cummings on Flo-Jo, and Sam Waters for the cover image. Thanks also to models who previously appeared in *The Usborne Complete Riding School*. Thanks to all at Aldborough Hall Equestrian Centre, Ilford; Pantile Hall, Brentwood; the Talland School of Equitation, Cirencester, and Rodeo Dave, Croydon, for the use of their facilities. Thanks to Janette Moss Horsewear, Waltham Abbey, for the use of saddlery.